Doggin'
America's Beaches

A Traveler's Guide To
Dog-Friendly Beaches –
(and those that aren't)

WITHDRAWN

DOUG GELBERT

illustrations by

ANDREW CHESWORTH

Cruden Bay Books

*There is always something for an active dog
to look forward to at the beach...*

DOGGIN' AMERICA'S BEACHES

Copyright 2007 by Cruden Bay Books

Cruden Bay Books
PO Box 467
Montchanin, DE 19710
www.hikewithyourdog.com

International Standard Book Number 978-0-9797074-4-5

"Dogs are our link to paradise...to sit with a dog on a hillside on a glorious afternoon is to be back in Eden, where doing nothing was not boring - it was peace."
- Milan Kundera

Ahead On The Trail

Also...

Introduction

It is hard to imagine any place a dog is happier than at a beach. Whether running around on the sand, jumping in the water or just lying in the sun, every dog deserves a day at the beach. But all too often dog owners stopping at a sandy stretch of beach are met with signs designed to make hearts - human and canine alike - droop: NO DOGS ON BEACH.

In *Doggin' America's Beaches* a beach regulation regarding dogs is listed for each beach. If the beach allows dogs at any time during the year, that rule is highlighted in **bold print**. Beaches that do not allow dogs are indicated by *italicized print*. The listed regulations are current as of the summer of 2007. As any dog owner knows, laws pertaining to dogs on the beach can literally change overnight - almost always to the detriment of sand-loving dogs. You can count on the topic of dogs being on the agenda at just about every government meeting in a beach community. So, if you are planning a special trip to a specific beach- call ahead. Did I miss your favorite? Let us know at *www.hikewithyourdog.com*.

The book lists American beaches in a rough circle from Maine to Florida, across to Texas, over to California, up to Washington and the the Great Lakes from Lake Superior east to Lake Ontario. Within each state the beaches are listed by region, if necessary. Within each region, the beaches are organized by town, which are listed alphabetically. If there is more than one beach in a town, the individual beaches are also listed alphabetically. If the state has only a few beaches and no regions, the beaches are not listed geographically from north to south but alphabetized by town as above. The only exception to these rules is that national seashores and lakeshores are always listed first and <u>underlined</u>.

Most beaches are listed by name and town with a phone number. Beaches are regulated by any one of a number of government agencies - town governments, county governments, state governments or federal governments. Since most beaches do not have phones, the numbers listed range from town halls to recreation departments to chambers of commerce to visitor centers. If someone at the other end of the line can't answer your beach question, they will no doubt be able to direct you to someone who can.

For dog owners it is sometimes hard to believe but not everyone loves dogs. We are, in fact, in the minority when compared with our non-dog owning neighbors. So when visiting a beach always keep your dog under control and clean up any messes and MAYBE more beaches will open to dogs. *Remember, every time you go out with your dog you are an ambassador for all dog owners.*

So the next time you plan a trip to the shore, don't forget to include the dog. Grab that leash and hit the beach!
DBG

Tips For Taking Your Dog To The Beach

- The majority of dogs can swim and love it, but dogs entering the water for the first time should be tested; never throw a dog into the water. Start in shallow water and call your dog's name - or try to coax him in with a treat or toy. Always keep your dog within reach.

- Another way to introduce your dog to the water is with a dog that already swims and is friendly with your dog. Let your dog follow his friend.

- If your dog begins to doggie paddle with his front legs only, lift his hind legs and help him float. He should quickly catch on and will keep his back end up.

- Swimming is a great form of exercise, but don't let your dog overdo it. He will be using new muscles and may tire quickly.

- Be careful of strong tides that are hazardous for even the best swimmers.

- Cool ocean water is tempting to your dog. Do not allow him to drink too much sea water. Salt in the water will make him sick. Salt and other minerals found in the ocean can damage your dog's coat so regular bathing is essential.

- Check with a lifeguard for daily water conditions - dogs are easy targets for jellyfish and sea lice.

- Dogs can get sunburned, especially short-haired dogs and ones with pink skin and white hair. Limit your dog's exposure when the sun is strong and apply sunblock to his ears and nose 30 minutes before going outside.

- If your dog is out of shape, don't encourage him to run on the sand, which is strenuous exercise and a dog that is out of shape can easily pull a tendon or ligament.

Your Dog On The Atlantic Coast Beaches...

Maine

Maine is known for its rocky coastline, especially in the northern stretches, but the many coves offer small sandy beaches in places. Maine is in the middle of the pack for dog-friendliness on its beaches. Dogs are not allowed on state beaches and you will have to wait until the off-season to take advantage of most of the town beaches.

Recommended Tail-Friendly Beaches

🐾 **York Harbor Beach.** A big, convenient parking lot next to a wide sand beach in a sheltered cove. You have to arrive early or come late in the summer but your dog can play here under voice control.

🐾 **Old Orchard Beach.** A classic resort beach with plenty of white sand and a long fishing pier. No dogs allowed on the beach mid-day during the summer but you don't have to get off the beach until 10:00 a.m.

🐾 **Drakes Island Beach.** Wells is a dog-friendly place with several beaches. Drakes Island is a wonderful, secluded choice.

DOWNEAST/ACADIA

Bar Harbor
207-288-3338

Acadia National Park
NO DOGS ON BEACH BUT ALLOWED ON TRAILS

Boothbay Harbor
207-633-2353

Barrett Park
LEASHED DOGS ALLOWED ON BEACH
Grimes Cove Beach
LEASHED DOGS ALLOWED ON BEACH

Castine
207-326-4502

Back Shore Beach
DOGS ALLOWED ON BEACH UNDER VOICE CONTROL OR ON A LEASH

Dennysville
207-726-4412

Cobscook Bay State Park
NO DOGS ON BEACH

Eastport
207-941-4014

Shackford Head State Park
NO DOGS ON BEACH

Lamoine 207-667-2242	Lamoine Beach **LEASHED DOGS ALLOWED ON BEACH**
Lubec 207-941-4014	Quoddy Head State Park **DOGS ALLOWED ON CARRYING PLACE COVE BEACH OUTSIDE PARK**
Rogue Bluffs 207-255-3475	Rogue Bluffs State Park *NO DOGS ALLOWED ON BEACH*
Seal Harbor 207-276-5531	Town Beach **DOGS ALLOWED ON BEACH OCT 15 TO MAY 15**
Stockton Springs 207-567-3404	Sandy Point Beach **DOGS ALLOWED ON BEACH**

MIDCOAST

Brunswick 207-725-6009	Thomas Point Beach **NO DOGS ALLOWED ON BEACH DURING EVENTS**
Georgetown 207-371-2303	Reid State Park *NO DOGS ALLOWED ON BEACH*
Owls Head 207-941-4014	Birch Point State Park *NO DOGS ALLOWED ON BEACH*
Phippsburg 207-389-1335	Popham Beach State Park *NO DOGS ALLOWED ON BEACH* Town Beach **DOGS ALLOWED ON BEACH**
Richmond 207-582-2813	Peacock Beach State Park *NO DOGS ALLOWED ON BEACH*

GREATER PORTLAND

Cape Elizabeth 207-799-5871	Crescent Beach State Park *NO DOGS ALLOWED ON BEACH*
Portland 207-874-8793	East End Beach **DOGS UNDER VOICE CONTROL FROM DAY AFTER LABOR DAY TO DAY BEFORE MEMORIAL DAY; NO DOGS IN SUMMER**

Scarborough 207-283-0067 207-883-7778	Ferry Beach State Park *NO DOGS ALLOWED ON BEACH* Higgins Beach **DOGS ALLOWED ON BEACH EXCEPT** **MID-DAY DURING THE SUMMER** Pine Point Beach **DOGS ALLOWED ON BEACH EXCEPT** **MID-DAY DURING THE SUMMER**
207-883-2416	Scarborough Beach State Park *NO DOGS ON BEACH*
207-883-7778	Western Beach **DOGS ALLOWED ON BEACH EXCEPT** **MID-DAY DURING THE SUMMER**
South Portland 207-767-3201	Willard Beach **DOGS ALLOWED ON BEACH FROM OCT-** **APRIL AND MAY-SEPT BETWEEN 6 AM** **AND 9 AM**

SOUTHERN COAST

Biddeford 207-284-9307	Beach Avenue **LEASHED DOGS ALLOWED ON BEACH** **EXCEPT BETWEEN 9 AM - 8 PM FROM** **MAY 25 TO SEPT 15** Biddeford Pool **LEASHED DOGS ALLOWED ON BEACH** **EXCEPT BETWEEN 9 AM - 8 PM FROM** **MAY 25 TO SEPT 15** Fortunes Rocks Beach **LEASHED DOGS ALLOWED ON BEACH** **EXCEPT BETWEEN 9 AM - 8 PM FROM** **MAY 25 TO SEPT 15** Hills Beach **LEASHED DOGS ALLOWED ON BEACH** **EXCEPT BETWEEN 9 AM - 8 PM FROM** **MAY 25 TO SEPT 15** Rotary Beach Park **LEASHED DOGS ALLOWED ON BEACH** **EXCEPT BETWEEN 9 AM - 8 PM FROM** **MAY 25 TO SEPT 15**
Kennebunk 207-967-4243	Gooch's Beach **FROM DAY FOLLOWING LABOR DAY** **UNTIL JUNE 15 DOGS ALLOWED ANY** **TIME; OTHERWISE DOGS NOT** **ALLOWED ON BEACH 9 AM - 5 PM** Middle Beach **FROM DAY FOLLOWING LABOR DAY** **UNTIL JUNE 15 DOGS ALLOWED ANY** **TIME; OTHERWISE DOGS NOT** **ALLOWED ON BEACH 9 AM - 5 PM**

Kennebunk 207-967-4243	Mother's Beach **FROM DAY FOLLOWING LABOR DAY UNTIL JUNE 15 DOGS ALLOWED ANY TIME; OTHERWISE DOGS NOT ALLOWED ON BEACH 9 AM - 5 PM**
207-985-2102	Parson's Beach **FROM DAY FOLLOWING LABOR DAY UNTIL JUNE 15 DOGS ALLOWED ANY TIME; OTHERWISE DOGS NOT ALLOWED ON BEACH 9 AM - 5 PM**
Kennebunkport 207-967-4243	Arundel Beach **FROM DAY FOLLOWING LABOR DAY UNTIL JUNE 15 DOGS ALLOWED ANY TIME; OTHERWISE DOGS NOT ALLOWED ON BEACH 9 AM - 5 PM** Cleaves Cove Beach **FROM DAY FOLLOWING LABOR DAY UNTIL JUNE 15 DOGS ALLOWED ANY TIME; OTHERWISE DOGS NOT ALLOWED ON BEACH 9 AM - 5 PM** Colony Beach **FROM DAY FOLLOWING LABOR DAY UNTIL JUNE 15 DOGS ALLOWED ANY TIME; OTHERWISE DOGS NOT ALLOWED ON BEACH 9 AM - 5 PM** Goose Rocks Beach **FROM DAY FOLLOWING LABOR DAY UNTIL JUNE 15 DOGS ALLOWED ANY TIME; OTHERWISE DOGS NOT ALLOWED ON BEACH 9 AM - 5 PM**
Kittery 207-439-0452	Fort Foster Park **DOGS ALLOWED ON BEACH BEFORE 10 AM AND AFTER 5 PM** Seapoint Beach **DOGS ALLOWED ON BEACH BEFORE 10 AM AND AFTER 5 PM**
Ogunquit 207-646-5139	Foot Bridge Beach **NO DOGS MAY 1 TO OCTOBER 15** Moody Beach **NO DOGS MAY 1 TO OCTOBER 15** Ogunquit Beach **NO DOGS MAY 1 TO OCTOBER 15**
Old Orchard Beach 207-934-2500	Old Orchard Beach **DOGS ALLOWED ON BEACH EXCEPT MEMORIAL DAY TO LABOR DAY FROM 10 AM - 5 PM**

11

| Saco | Bayview Beach |
| 207-284-4831 | **LEASHED DOGS ALLOWED ON BEACH** |

Wells
207-646-5113

Drakes Island Beach
**FROM 6/16 TO 9/15 NO DOGS
ALLOWED ON BEACH FROM 8 AM TO
6 PM; BEFORE 8 AM AND AFTER 6 PM
UNDER CHARGE OF RESPONSIBLE
PERSON; ANYTIME FROM 9/16 TO 6/15**
Wells Beach
**FROM 6/16 TO 9/15 NO DOGS
ALLOWED ON BEACH FROM 8 AM TO
6 PM; BEFORE 8 AM AND AFTER 6 PM
UNDER CHARGE OF RESPONSIBLE
PERSON; ANYTIME FROM 9/16 TO 6/15**

York
207-363-1000

Cape Neddick Beach
**IN SUMMER NO DOGS ALLOWED ON
BEACH FROM 8 AM TO 6 PM; DOGS
WELCOME ANYTIME IN OFF-SEASON**
Harbor Beach
**IN SUMMER NO DOGS ALLOWED ON
BEACH FROM 8 AM TO 6 PM; DOGS
WELCOME ANYTIME IN OFF-SEASON**
Long Sands Beach
**IN SUMMER NO DOGS ALLOWED ON
BEACH FROM 8 AM TO 6 PM; DOGS
WELCOME ANYTIME IN OFF-SEASON**
Short Sands Beach
**IN SUMMER NO DOGS ALLOWED ON
BEACH FROM 8 AM TO 6 PM; DOGS
WELCOME ANYTIME IN OFF-SEASON**

*"My dog is worried about the economy because
Alpo is up to 99 cents a can. That's almost
$7.00 in dog money."*
-Joe Weinstein

New Hampshire

If you are taking the dog to New Hampshire, head for the mountains. The Granite State does not give dog owners much reason to stop when driving along its 18 miles of Atlantic Ocean shoreline.

Hampton	Hampton Beach
603-926-8718	*NO DOGS ALLOWED ON BEACH*
603-926-3784	Hampton Beach State Park
	NO DOGS ALLOWED ON BEACH
603-926-8718	North Beach
	NO DOGS ALLOWED ON BEACH
New Castle	Grand Island Common
603-431-6710	**NO DOGS ON BEACH FROM MAY 15 TO SEPT 15**
North Hampton	North Hampton State Beach
603-436-1552	*NO DOGS ALLOWED ON BEACH*
Rye	Foss Beach
603-964-6281	**DOGS ALLOWED ON BEACH FROM OCT 1 TO THE SATURDAY BEFORE MEMORIAL DAY: BEFORE 8 AM AND AFTER 6 PM OTHERWISE**
603-436-1552	Jenness State Beach
	NO DOGS ALLOWED ON BEACH
603-436-9404	Wallis Sands State Beach
	NO DOGS ALLOWED ON BEACH
Seabrook	Seabrook Beach
603-474-3871	*NO DOGS ALLOWED ON BEACH*

"Dogs' lives are too short. Their only fault, really."
-Agnes Sligh Turnbull

13

Massachusetts

Massachusetts is the best northeastern state to take your dog to the beach in summer. The resort islands are particularly dog-friendly and several spots on Cape Cod will permit dogs in non-swimming areas. The beaches around Boston are generally restrictive until the off-season.

Recommended Tail-Friendly Beaches

🐾 **Cape Cod National Seashore.** Dogs are allowed on all non-nesting protected beaches year-round. Walking the beaches at Cape Cod is a special experience due to limited sight distance down the shore caused by the curvature of the coastline. The effect is that of a series of private beaches as you move from beach alcove to beach alcove. In addition to Atlantic Ocean beaches backed by impressive highlands, the park extends across the cape to include bayside beaches with gentler waves for doggie swims.

🐾 **Nantucket Island.** Dogs are allowed on island beaches the entire year, although there are restrictions during the summer. Dogs are even allowed on the shuttle buses to the beach.

NORTH SHORE

Beverly	Brackenberry Beach
978-921-6067	**NO DOGS ON BEACH MEMORIAL DAY-LABOR DAY**
	Dane Street Beach
	NO DOGS ON BEACH MEMORIAL DAY-LABOR DAY
	Independence Park
	NO DOGS ON BEACH MEMORIAL DAY-LABOR DAY
	Lynch Park Beach
	NO DOGS ON BEACH MEMORIAL DAY-LABOR DAY
	Pleasant View Beach
	NO DOGS ON BEACH MEMORIAL DAY-LABOR DAY
	Woodbury Beach
	NO DOGS ON BEACH MEMORIAL DAY-LABOR DAY

Danvers 978-777-0001	Sandy Beach **LEASHED DOGS ALLOWED ON BEACH**
Gloucester 800-649-6839	Cressey's Beach **NO DOGS ON BEACH MEMORIAL DAY- LABOR DAY** Good Harbor Beach **NO DOGS ON BEACH MEMORIAL DAY- LABOR DAY** Half Moon Beach **NO DOGS ON BEACH MEMORIAL DAY- LABOR DAY** Niles Beach **NO DOGS ON BEACH MEMORIAL DAY- LABOR DAY** Stage Fort Beach **NO DOGS ON BEACH MEMORIAL DAY- LABOR DAY** Wingaersheek Beach **NO DOGS ON BEACH MEMORIAL DAY- LABOR DAY**
Ipswich 978-356-4351	Crane Beach **NO DOGS ON BEACH IN SUMMER**
Lynn 781-598-4000 617-727-1397 781-598-4000	Lynn Beach **NO DOGS ON BEACH MEMORIAL DAY- LABOR DAY** Lynn Shores Reservation **NO DOGS ON BEACH IN SWIMMING AREAS** Pavilion Beach **NO DOGS ON BEACH MEMORIAL DAY- LABOR DAY**
Manchester 978-526-2000	Black & White Beaches **NO DOGS ON BEACH MAY 1 TO OCT 1** Singing Beach **NO DOGS ON BEACH MAY 1 TO OCT 1**
Marblehead 781-631-0000	Devereux Beach **NO DOGS ON BEACH MAY TO SEPT** Grace Oliver Beach **NO DOGS ON BEACH MAY TO SEPT**
Nahant 617-581-0018	Forty Steps Beach **NO DOGS ON BEACH MAY TO SEPT 30** Long Beach **NO DOGS ON BEACH MAY TO SEPT 30** Short Beach **NO DOGS ON BEACH MAY TO SEPT 30** Tudor Beach **NO DOGS ON BEACH MAY TO SEPT 30**

Newburyport	Plum Island Beach
978-465-5753	**NO DOGS ON BEACH APRIL 1 TO OCT 1**

Revere	Revere Beach
617-727-8856	*NO DOGS ON BEACH*

Rockport	Back and Front Beaches
978-546-6894	**NO DOGS ON BEACH JUNE 1 TO SEPT 15**
	Cape Hedge
	NO DOGS ON BEACH JUNE 1 TO SEPT 15
	Halibut Point
	DOGS ALLOWED ON BEACH
	Old Garden Beach
	NO DOGS ON BEACH JUNE 1 TO SEPT 15
	Pebble Beach
	NO DOGS ON BEACH JUNE 1 TO SEPT 15

Salem	Collins Cove
978-745-0241	**LEASHED DOGS ALLOWED ON BEACH**
	Willows Beach
	LEASHED DOGS ALLOWED ON BEACH
	Winter Island
	NO DOGS ON BEACH

Salisbury	Salisbury State Reservation
978-462-4481	**DOGS ALLOWED ON BEACH FROM DAY AFTER COLUMBUS DAY TO DAY BEFORE PATRIOT'S DAY**
978-465-3581	Salisbury Town Beach
	NO DOGS ALLOWED ON BEACH IN SUMMER

Swampscott	Fishermen's Beach
781-596-8854	**DOGS ALLOWED ON BEACH OCT 1 TO MAY 20**
	King's Beach
	DOGS ALLOWED ON BEACH OCT 1 TO MAY 20
	Phillips Beach
	DOGS ALLOWED ON BEACH OCT 1 TO MAY 20
	Preston Beach
	DOGS ALLOWED ON BEACH OCT 1 TO MAY 20
	Whale's Beach
	DOGS ALLOWED ON BEACH OCT 1 TO MAY 20

SOUTH SHORE

<u>Boston Harbor Islands National Park</u>
617-223-8666   *NO DOGS ALLOWED ON BEACH*

Boston   Dorchester Shores Reservation
617-727-6034   *NO DOGS ON BEACH IN SWIMMING AREA*

Hull   Nantasket Beach Reservation
617-727-8856   *NO DOGS ON BEACH IN SWIMMING AREA*

Plymouth   Duxbury Beach
508-830-4095   **LEASHED DOGS ALLOWED ON BEACH**
                    Nelson Beach
                    LEASHED DOGS ALLOWED ON BEACH
                    Plymouth's Long Beach
                    LEASHED DOGS ALLOWED ON BEACH

Quincy   Quincy Shore Reservation
617-727-5293   *NO DOGS ON BEACH IN SWIMMING AREA*

Scituate   Egypt Beach
781-545-8704   **NO DOGS ON BEACH 10 AM - 6 PM**
                    FROM JUNE 15 TO SEPT 15
                    Humarock Beach
                    NO DOGS ON BEACH 10 AM - 6 PM
                    FROM JUNE 15 TO SEPT 15
                    Minot Beach
                    NO DOGS ON BEACH 10 AM - 6 PM
                    FROM JUNE 15 TO SEPT 15
                    Peggotty Beach
                    NO DOGS ON BEACH 10 AM - 6 PM
                    FROM JUNE 15 TO SEPT 15
                    Sand Hills Beach
                    NO DOGS ON BEACH 10 AM - 6 PM
                    FROM JUNE 15 TO SEPT 15

*"My dog can bark like a Congressman, fetch like an aide,
beg like a press secretary and play dead
like a receptionist."*
          -Gerald Solomon

CAPE COD

Cape Cod National Seashore
508-487-1256   **DOGS ALLOWED ON BEACH ANYTIME BUT NOT IN LIFEGUARDED SWIMMING AREAS, NATURE TRAILS OR BIRD NESTING AREAS**

Barnstable   Craigville Beach
877-492-6647   **DOGS ALLOWED ON BEACH SEPT 15 - MAY 15**
                  Kalmus Park Beach
                  DOGS ALLOWED ON BEACH SEPT 15 - MAY 15
                  Orrin Keyes Beach
                  DOGS ALLOWED ON BEACH SEPT 15 - MAY 15
                  Sandy Neck Beach
                  DOGS ALLOWED ON BEACH SEPT 15 - MAY 15
                  Veterans Beach
                  DOGS ALLOWED ON BEACH SEPT 15 - MAY 15

Bourne   Monument Beach
508-759-6000   *NO DOGS ALLOWED ON BEACH*

Brewster   Breakwater Beach
508-896-3500   **DOGS ON BEACH OCT 1 - MEMORIAL DAY**
                  Paine's Creek Beach
                  DOGS ON BEACH OCT 1 - MEMORIAL DAY
                  Robbins Hill Beach
                  DOGS ON BEACH OCT 1 - MEMORIAL DAY

Chatham   Cockle Cove Beach
508-945-5199   **DOGS ALLOWED ON BEACH SEPT 16 - MAY 14**
                  Forest Beach
                  DOGS ALLOWED ON BEACH SEPT 16 - MAY 14
                  Hardings Beach
                  DOGS ALLOWED ON BEACH SEPT 16 - MAY 14
                  Ridgevale Beach
                  DOGS ALLOWED ON BEACH SEPT 16 - MAY 14

| Dennis
508-394-8300 | Chapin Memorial Beach
DOGS ON BEACH LABOR DAY -
MEMORIAL DAY
Corporation Road Beach
DOGS ON BEACH LABOR DAY -
MEMORIAL DAY
Glendon Road Beach
DOGS ON BEACH LABOR DAY -
MEMORIAL DAY
Haigis Beach
DOGS ON BEACH LABOR DAY -
MEMORIAL DAY
Horsefoot Path Beach
DOGS ON BEACH LABOR DAY -
MEMORIAL DAY
Howes Street Beach
DOGS ON BEACH LABOR DAY -
MEMORIAL DAY
Inman Road Beach
DOGS ON BEACH LABOR DAY -
MEMORIAL DAY
Mayflower Beach
DOGS ON BEACH LABOR DAY -
MEMORIAL DAY
Raycroft Parking Beach
DOGS ON BEACH LABOR DAY -
MEMORIAL DAY
Sea Street Beach
DOGS ON BEACH LABOR DAY -
MEMORIAL DAY
South Village Road Beach
DOGS ON BEACH LABOR DAY -
MEMORIAL DAY
West Dennis Beach
DOGS ON BEACH LABOR DAY -
MEMORIAL DAY |
| Eastham
508-240-7211 | Campground Beach
DOGS ON BEACH LABOR DAY TO FLAG DAY
Coast Guard Beach
DOGS ON BEACH LABOR DAY TO FLAG DAY
Cooks Brook Beach
DOGS ON BEACH LABOR DAY TO FLAG DAY
First Encounter Beach
DOGS ON BEACH LABOR DAY TO FLAG DAY
Nauset Light Beach
DOGS ON BEACH OUTSIDE SWIMMING
AREAS
Sunken Meadow Beach
DOGS ON BEACH LABOR DAY TO FLAG DAY
Thumpertown Beach
DOGS ON BEACH LABOR DAY TO FLAG DAY |

Falmouth
800-526-8532

Bristol Beach
**DOGS ALLOWED ON BEACH ALL YEAR
EXCEPT DURING "BEACH HOURS"**
Chapoquoit Beach
**DOGS ALLOWED ON BEACH ALL YEAR
EXCEPT DURING "BEACH HOURS"**
Falmouth Heights Beach
**DOGS ALLOWED ON BEACH ALL YEAR
EXCEPT DURING "BEACH HOURS"**
Megansett Beach
**DOGS ALLOWED ON BEACH ALL YEAR
EXCEPT DURING "BEACH HOURS"**
Menauhant Beach
**DOGS ALLOWED ON BEACH ALL YEAR
EXCEPT DURING "BEACH HOURS"**
Old Silver Beach
**DOGS ALLOWED ON BEACH ALL YEAR
EXCEPT DURING "BEACH HOURS"**
Stoney Beach
**DOGS ALLOWED ON BEACH ALL YEAR
EXCEPT DURING "BEACH HOURS"**
Surf Drive Beach
**DOGS ALLOWED ON BEACH ALL YEAR
EXCEPT DURING "BEACH HOURS"**
Trunk River Beach
**DOGS ALLOWED ON BEACH ALL YEAR
EXCEPT DURING "BEACH HOURS"**
Wood Heck Beach
**DOGS ALLOWED ON BEACH ALL YEAR
EXCEPT DURING "BEACH HOURS"**

Harwich
800-442-7942

Bank Street Beach
**DOGS ALLOWED ON BEACH OCT 1 TO
MAY 14**
Jenkins Beach
**DOGS ALLOWED ON BEACH OCT 1 TO
MAY 14**
Merkle Beach
**DOGS ALLOWED ON BEACH OCT 1 TO
MAY 14**
Pleasant Road Beach
**DOGS ALLOWED ON BEACH OCT 1 TO
MAY 14**
Red River Beach
**DOGS ALLOWED ON BEACH OCT 1 TO
MAY 14**

Mashpee
508-477-0792

South Cape Beach
NO DOGS ALLOWED ON BEACH

Orleans 800-865-1386	Nauset Beach **NO DOGS MEMORIAL DAY - LABOR DAY** Pleasant Bay Beach **NO DOGS MEMORIAL DAY - LABOR DAY** Rock Harbor Beach **NO DOGS MEMORIAL DAY - LABOR DAY** Skaket Beach **NO DOGS MEMORIAL DAY - LABOR DAY**
Provincetown/Herring Cove 508-487-3424	**DOGS ON BEACH EXCEPT IN SWIMMING AREAS** Race Point **DOGS ON BEACH EXCEPT IN SWIMMING AREAS** Town Beach **DOGS ON BEACH EXCEPT IN SWIMMING AREAS**
Sandwich	East Sandwich Beach **NO DOGS ON BEACH MAY 15 - SEPT 15** Scusset Beach **NO DOGS ON BEACH MAY 15 - SEPT 15** Town Neck Beach **NO DOGS ON BEACH MAY 15 - SEPT 15**
Truro 508-487-1288	Ballston Beach **LEASHED DOGS ALLOWED ON BEACH EXCEPT JULY AND AUGUST 9 AM - 5 PM** Coast Guard Beach **LEASHED DOGS ALLOWED ON BEACH EXCEPT JULY AND AUGUST 9 AM - 5 PM** Corn Hill Beach **LEASHED DOGS ALLOWED ON BEACH EXCEPT JULY AND AUGUST 9 AM - 5 PM** Fisher Beach **LEASHED DOGS ALLOWED ON BEACH EXCEPT JULY AND AUGUST 9 AM - 5 PM** Great Hollow Beach **LEASHED DOGS ALLOWED ON BEACH EXCEPT JULY AND AUGUST 9 AM - 5 PM** Head of Meadow Beach **LEASHED DOGS ALLOWED ON BEACH EXCEPT JULY AND AUGUST 9 AM - 5 PM** Longnook Beach **LEASHED DOGS ALLOWED ON BEACH EXCEPT JULY AND AUGUST 9 AM - 5 PM** Ryder Beach **LEASHED DOGS ALLOWED ON BEACH EXCEPT JULY AND AUGUST 9 AM - 5 PM**

Wareham 508-291-3140	Briarwood Beach **DOGS ON BEACH BETWEEN 5:01 PM and 7:59 AM** Hamilton Beach **DOGS ON BEACH BETWEEN 5:01 PM and 7:59 AM** Little Harbor Beach **DOGS ON BEACH BETWEEN 5:01 PM and 7:59 AM** Long Beach **DOGS ON BEACH BETWEEN 5:01 PM and 7:59 AM** Parkwood Beach **DOGS ON BEACH BETWEEN 5:01 PM and 7:59 AM** Pinehurst Beach **DOGS ON BEACH BETWEEN 5:01 PM and 7:59 AM** Swifts Beach **DOGS ON BEACH BETWEEN 5:01 PM and 7:59 AM**
Wellfleet 508-349-9818	Cahoon Hollow Beach **DOGS ALLOWED ON BEACH BEFORE 9 AM AND AFTER 5 PM FROM SATURDAY PRIOR TO JULY 1 THROUGH LABOR DAY; ANYTIME OTHERWISE** Marconi Beach **DOGS ON BEACH OUTSIDE SWIMMING AREAS** White Crest Beach **DOGS ALLOWED ON BEACH BEFORE 9 AM AND AFTER 5 PM FROM SATURDAY PRIOR TO JULY 1 THROUGH LABOR DAY; ANYTIME OTHERWISE**
Yarmouth 508-398-2231	Bass Hole Beach *NO DOGS ALLOWED ON BEACH* Bay View Beach *NO DOGS ALLOWED ON BEACH* Eagle View Beach *NO DOGS ALLOWED ON BEACH* Parkers River Beach *NO DOGS ALLOWED ON BEACH* Seagull Beach *NO DOGS ALLOWED ON BEACH* Seaview Beach *NO DOGS ALLOWED ON BEACH* Windmill Beach *NO DOGS ALLOWED ON BEACH*

THE ISLANDS

Martha's Vineyard

Aquinnah
508-645-2300

Lobsterstown Beach
NO DOGS ALLOWED ON BEACH
Moshup (Gay Head) Beach
NO DOGS ALLOWED ON BEACH
Philbin Beach
NO DOGS ALLOWED ON BEACH

Edgartown
508-627-1000

East Beach
DOGS ALLOWED ON BEACH IN OFF-SEASON
Katama Beach
DOGS ALLOWED ON BEACH IN OFF-SEASON
Norton Point Beach
DOGS ARE ALLOWED ON BEACH AT ALL TIMES EXCEPT BETWEEN MAY 15 AND SEPT 15 FROM THE HOURS OF 8 AM TO 6 PM; DOGS MUST ALSO BE KEPT 100 YARDS FROM POSTED BIRD NESTING AREAS
Lighthouse Beach
DOGS ALLOWED ON BEACH IN OFF-SEASON
South Beach
DOGS ALLOWED ON BEACH IN OFF-SEASON

Menemsha
508-693-0085

Menemsha Public Beach
DOGS ALLOWED ON BEACH IN OFF-SEASON

"Money will buy a pretty good dog but it won't buy the wag of his tail."
-Josh Billings

Oak Bluffs
508-693-5511

Eastville Point Beach
DOGS ARE ALLOWED ON BEACH AT ALL TIMES EXCEPT BETWEEN MAY 15 AND SEPT 15 FROM THE HOURS OF 8 AM TO 6 PM; DOGS MUST ALSO BE KEPT 100 YARDS FROM POSTED BIRD NESTING AREAS

Joseph Sylvia Sate Beach
DOGS ARE ALLOWED ON BEACH AT ALL TIMES EXCEPT BETWEEN MAY 15 AND SEPT 15 FROM THE HOURS OF 8 AM TO 6 PM; DOGS MUST ALSO BE KEPT 100 YARDS FROM POSTED BIRD NESTING AREAS

Town Beach
DOGS ARE ALLOWED ON BEACH AT ALL TIMES EXCEPT BETWEEN MAY 15 AND SEPT 15 FROM THE HOURS OF 8 AM TO 6 PM; DOGS MUST ALSO BE KEPT 100 YARDS FROM POSTED BIRD NESTING AREAS

Vineyard Haven
508-696-4200

Owen Park Beach
DOGS ALLOWED ON BEACH IN OFF-SEASON

Nantucket Island

Brandt Point Beach
Children's Beach
Cisco Beach
Dionis Beach
Francis Street Beach
Jetties Beach
Madaket Beach
Miacomet Beach
Siasconet Beach
Surfside Beach
NANTUCKET IS A VERY DOG-FRIENDLY ISLAND; GENERALLY DOGS ARE NOT ALLOWED IN SWIMMING AREAS OF THE BEACHES AND HOURS ARE RESTRICTED DURING MID-DAY IN THE BUSY SUMMER SEASON; DOGS ARE ALSO WELCOME ON BEACH SHUTTLE BUSES

SOUTH COAST

Dartmouth	Apponagansett Beach
508-910-1812	*NO DOGS ALLOWED ON THE BEACH*
508-636-8816	Demarest Lloyd State Park
	DOGS NOT ALLOWED IN THE SWIMMING AREAS
508-910-1812	Jones Park
	NO DOGS ALLOWED ON BEACH
508-910-1812	Round Hill
	RESIDENTS ONLY BEACH
Fairhaven	Fort Phoenix State Reservation
508-992-4524	*DOGS NOT ALLOWED IN THE SWIMMING AREAS*
508-979-4025	West Island Town Beach
	DOGS ALLOWED ON BEACH
Marion	Silver Shell Beach
508-748-3502	*NO DOGS ALLOWED ON THE BEACH*
Mattapoisett	Town Beach (Aucott Road)
508-758-4103	**DOGS ALLOWED ON THE BEACH**
	Town Beach (Water Street)
	DOGS ALLOWED ON THE BEACH
New Bedford	East Beach
508-979-1450	*NO DOGS ALLOWED ON BEACH*
	West Beach
	NO DOGS ALLOWED ON BEACH
Westport	Cherry & Webb Beach
508-616-1000	**DOGS ON BEACH FROM NOV 1 TO APRIL 1**
	East Beach
	DOGS ON BEACH FROM NOV 1 TO APRIL 1
	Horseneck Beach State Reservation
	NO DOGS ALLOWED IN THE SWIMMING AREAS

Rhode Island

With some 400 miles of shoreline within a short drive your wave-loving dog can enjoy a salt-water swim somewhere any time of the year - even in the summer. If you are in the Ocean State in the summer, get out to Block Island where dogs are welcome on the beach all year-round.

Recommended Tail-Friendly Beaches

- **Scarborough State Beach.** Rhode Island's biggest sand beach in Narragansett is off-limits from early May through Labor Day but your dog will want to line up on that first Tuesday in September to romp on this long, wide stretch of white sand.

- **Block Island.** There are 17 miles of public beaches on Block Island so your dog will get an ocean swim - although it will take a hike of several miles to reach some of the more dramatic sand beneath the cliffs. Crescent Beach, a few pawprints from the ferry landing, is the most convenient but crowded in-season. One beach that is too small for sun worshippers but ideal for dogs is just south of Old Harbor along Spring Street - as you reach the crest of a hill drop down to the sand in front of a guardrail for great canine swimming along a breakwater in frisky waves.

- **Cliff Walk.** The famous path through America's most spectacular backyard is open to dogs. In the off-season your dog can enjoy a 3/4-mile swath of sand on First Beach at the beginning of the Cliff Walk or anytime on Reject Beach deep into the Walk.

NARRAGANSETT BAY

Barrington 401-274-1925	Town Beach *NO DOGS ALLOWED*
Bristol 401-253-7000	Town Beach **DOGS ALLOWED YEAR-ROUND**
Jamestown 401-884-2010 401-423-7260	Beavertail State Park **NO DOGS ON BEACH IN SUMMER** Heads Beach/Mackarel Cove/Town Beach **NO DOGS ON BEACH MEMORIAL DAY TO LABOR DAY**

Little Compton 401-635-9974	South Shore Beach **DOGS ALLOWED ON BEACH WHEN SWIMMING AREA IS CLOSED**
Middletown 401-847-2750	Atlantic Beach **NO DOGS ON BEACH MEMORIAL DAY-LABOR DAY** Second Beach/Sachuset Town Beach **NO DOGS ON BEACH MEMORIAL DAY-LABOR DAY**
401-847-2750	Third Beach **NO DOGS ON BEACH MEMORIAL DAY-LABOR DAY**
Newport 401-845-5810	Easton's Beach/First Beach **NO DOGS ON BEACH MEMORIAL DAY-LABOR DAY** Fort Adams State Park *NO DOGS ALLOWED* Kings Park Beach **NO DOGS ON BEACH MEMORIAL DAY-LABOR DAY**
Portsmouth 401-683-2101	Island Park Beach **NO DOGS ON BEACH MEMORIAL DAY-LABOR DAY** Sandy Point Beach **DOGS ALLOWED ON BEACH YEAR-ROUND** Teddy's Beach **DOGS ALLOWED ON BEACH YEAR-ROUND**
Tiverton 401-625-6780	Fogland Beach **NO DOGS ON BEACH MEMORIAL DAY-LABOR DAY** Grinnell's Beach **DOGS ALLOWED ON BEACH YEAR-ROUND**
Warwick 401-738-2000	Buttonwoods Beach **NO DOGS ON BEACH MEMORIAL DAY-LABOR DAY** Conimicut Point Beach **NO DOGS ON BEACH MEMORIAL DAY-LABOR DAY**
401-884-2010	Goddard Memorial State Beach **NO DOGS ON BEACH MEMORIAL DAY-LABOR DAY**
401-738-2000	Oakland Beach **NO DOGS ON BEACH MEMORIAL DAY-LABOR DAY**
Warren 401-245-0200	Town Beach *NO DOGS ALLOWED*

BLOCK ISLAND

Block Island
401-466-7717

Crescent Beach/Fred Benson Town Beach
DOGS ALLOWED ON BEACH YEAR-ROUND
North Light

401-466-3200
DOGS ALLOWED ON BEACH YEAR-ROUND

New Shoreham

Charleston Beach
DOGS ALLOWED ON BEACH YEAR-ROUND
Mansion Beach
DOGS ALLOWED ON BEACH YEAR-ROUND

ATLANTIC OCEAN

Charleston
401-322-8910
401-364-7000

East Beach
DOGS ALLOWED OCTOBER - APRIL
Town Beach
**NO DOGS ON BEACH MEMORIAL DAY-
LABOR DAY**

Matunuck
401-789-9301

South Kingstown Town Beach
DOGS ALLOWED OCTOBER - APRIL

Narragansett
401-789-8374

Salty Brine State Park
**NO DOGS ON BEACH MEMORIAL DAY-
LABOR DAY**
Scarborough State Park
**NO DOGS ON BEACH MEMORIAL DAY-
LABOR DAY**

401-789-1044
Town Beach
**NO DOGS ON BEACH MEMORIAL DAY-
LABOR DAY**

South Kingstown
401-789-8374
401-783-7416

East Matunuck State Beach
DOGS ALLOWED OCTOBER - APRIL
Roy Carpenter's Beach
**NO DOGS ON BEACH MEMORIAL DAY-
LABOR DAY**

Watch Hill

Watch Hill Beach
DOGS ALLOWED ON BEACH YEAR-ROUND

Westerly
401-364-1206

Blue Shutters Town Beach
**NO DOGS ON BEACH MEMORIAL DAY-
LABOR DAY**

401-596-9097
Misquamicut State Beach
**NO DOGS ON BEACH MEMORIAL DAY-
LABOR DAY**
Napatree Point
DOGS ALLOWED ON BEACH YEAR-ROUND

Connecticut

The sandy beaches of the Nutmeg State on Long Island Sound are not known for being dog-friendly. But many aren't that friendly to people either, with restricted access being common when you arrive.

Clinton
203-669-6901

Town Beach
NO DOGS ALLOWED ON BEACH

East Haven
203-468-3367

Town Beach
DOGS ALLOWED ON BEACH FROM LABOR DAY TO MEMORIAL DAY

East Lyme
860-739-5471

Rocky Neck State Park
DOGS NOT ALLOWED ON BEACH

Fairfield
203-256-3000

Jennings Beach
DOGS ON BEACH FROM OCT 1 - APRIL 1
Penfield Beach
DOGS ON BEACH FROM OCT 1 - APRIL 1
Richards Beach
DOGS ON BEACH FROM OCT 1 - APRIL 1
Sasco Beach
DOGS ON BEACH FROM OCT 1 - APRIL 1
Southport Beach
DOGS ON BEACH FROM OCT 1 - APRIL 1

Groton
860-536-5680

Bluff Point Park
DOGS ALLOWED ON BEACH
Esker Point Beach
 DOGS ALLOWED ON BEACH EXCEPT DURING NIGHTS WITH CONCERTS
Main Street Beach
DOGS ALLOWED ON BEACH

Madison
203-245-5623
203-245-1817

203-245-5623

203-245-5623

East Wharf Beach
NO DOGS ALLOWED ON BEACH
Hammonasset Beach State Park
NO DOGS ALLOWED ON BEACH
Surf Club Beach
NO DOGS ALLOWED ON BEACH
West Wharf Beach
NO DOGS ALLOWED ON BEACH

Milford	Gulf Beach
203-783-3201	*NO DOGS ALLOWED ON BEACH*
203-735-4311	Silver Sands State Beach
	NO DOGS ALLOWED ON BEACH
203-783-3201	Walnut Beach
	NO DOGS ALLOWED ON BEACH
New Haven	Lighthouse Point Park
203-946-8790	*NO DOGS ALLOWED ON BEACH*
New London	Ocean Beach Park
800-510-7263	*NO DOGS ALLOWED ON BEACH*
Old Lyme	Sound View Beach
860-434-1605 x235	*NO DOGS ALLOWED ON BEACH*
Old Saybrook	Harvey's Beach
860-395-3123	*NO DOGS ALLOWED ON BEACH*
	Town Beach
	NO DOGS ALLOWED ON BEACH
Stamford	Cove Island Park
203-977-4054	*NON-RESIDENTS ARE DISCOURAGED FROM USING THE BEACH*
	Cummings Park
	NON-RESIDENTS ARE DISCOURAGED FROM USING THE BEACH
Stonington	Dubois Beach
860-535-5060	*NO DOGS ALLOWED ON BEACH*
Stratford	Long Beach
203-385-4020	*NO DOGS ALLOWED ON BEACH*
	Russian Beach
	NO DOGS ALLOWED ON BEACH
	Short Beach Park
	NO DOGS ALLOWED ON BEACH
West Haven	Altschuler Beach
203-937-3651	*NO DOGS ALLOWED ON BEACH*
	Bradley Point Park
	NO DOGS ALLOWED ON BEACH
	Dawson Beach
	NO DOGS ALLOWED ON BEACH
	Morse Beach
	NO DOGS ALLOWED ON BEACH
	Oak Street Beach
	NO DOGS ALLOWED ON BEACH
	Peck Beach
	NO DOGS ALLOWED ON BEACH
	Seabluff Beach
	NO DOGS ALLOWED ON BEACH

Westport
203-341-1038

Burying Hill Beach
DOGS ALLOWED ON BEACH NOV 1 TO APR 30
Canal Beach
DOGS ALLOWED ON BEACH NOV 1 TO APR 30
Compo Beach
DOGS ALLOWED ON BEACH NOV 1 TO APR 30
Old Mill Beach
DOGS ALLOWED ON BEACH NOV 1 TO APR 30
Sherwood Island State Park
LEASHED DOGS ALLOWED IN PARK OCT 1 TO APRIL 14

How To Pet A Dog
Tickling tummies slowly and gently works wonders.
Never use a rubbing motion; this makes dogs bad-tempered.
A gentle tickle with the tips of the fingers is all that is necessary
to induce calm in a dog. I hate strangers who go up to dogs with
their hands held to the dog's nose, usually palm towards themselves.
How does the dog know that the hand doesn't hold something hor-
rid? The palm should always be shown to the dog and go straight
down to between the dog's front legs and tickle gently with
a soothing voice to accompany the action.
Very often the dog raises its back leg in a scratching movement,
it gets so much pleasure from this.
-Barbara Woodhouse

New York

The further east you go out on Long Island the more dog-friendly New York becomes but whether on the north shore or south shore your dog is going to need to wait until the off-season to really sample the Long Island Sound or Atlantic Ocean.

Recommended Tail-Friendly Beaches

- **Montauk.** The many beaches, some stone and some sandy, will welcome dogs if you stay out of the swimming areas. The town beaches are very tail-friendly and Hither Hills State Park and Theodore Roosevelt County Park offer geat trails before you reach the beach.

- **The Hamptons.** Come in the winter and you dog will have these magnificent Atlantic Ocean beaches to herself.

NASSAU COUNTY - NORTH SHORE

Bayville 516-628-1439	Creek Beach *BEACH FOR RESIDENT DOGS ONLY*
Port Washington 516-883-6566 516-766-1029	Bar Beach Park *NO DOGS ALLOWED ON BEACH* Hempstead Harbor Beach Park *NO DOGS ALLOWED ON BEACH*
516-883-6566	Manorhaven Beach Park *NO DOGS ALLOWED ON BEACH*

NASSAU COUNTY - SOUTH SHORE

Lido 516-571-7700	Nassau Beach Park **DOGS ALLOWED ON BEACH EXCEPT WHEN BIRDS ARE NESTING**
Wantaugh 516-785-1600	Jones Beach *NO DOGS ALLOWED ON BEACH*

SUFFOLK COUNTY - NORTH SHORE

Centerport
516-754-9537
516-351-9481

Centerport Beach
NO DOGS ALLOWED ON BEACH
Fleets Cove Beach
NO DOGS ALLOWED ON BEACH
Seniors Beach (seniors only)

516-754-9537

NO DOGS ALLOWED ON BEACH

Eatons Neck
631-261-7574

Asharoken Beach
NO DOGS ALLOWED ON BEACH

Huntington
516-423-0014
516-351-9289

Crescent Beach
NO DOGS ALLOWED ON BEACH
Gold Star Battalion Beach
NO DOGS ALLOWED ON BEACH

516-351-9565

West Neck Beach
NO DOGS ALLOWED ON BEACH

Kings Park
631-269-4333

Sunken Meadow State Park
NO DOGS ALLOWED ON BEACH

Lloyd Harbor
516-423-1770

Caumesett State Park
NO DOGS ALLOWED ON BEACH

Wading River
631-727-5744
631-929-4314

Wading River Beach
NO DOGS ALLOWED ON BEACH
Wildwood State Park
NO DOGS ALLOWED ON BEACH

SUFFOLK COUNTY - EASTERN FORKS

Amagansett
631-324-4143

Alberts Landing Beach
LOCAL RESIDENT DOGS ONLY IN SEASON
Atlantic Avenue Beach
DOGS ALLOWED ON BEACH IN OFF-SEASON
Indian Wells Beach
LOCAL RESIDENT DOGS ONLY IN SEASON

Bridgehampton
631-283-6011

Mecox Beach
LOCAL RESIDENT DOGS ONLY IN SEASON
W. Scott Cameron Beach
LOCAL RESIDENT DOGS ONLY IN SEASON

East Hampton
631-324-4140

Town Beaches
NO DOGS ON BEACH BETWEEN 10 AM - 6 PM BETWEEN MAY 15 AND SEPT 15

Montauk 631-668-5081	Ditch Plains Beach **DOGS ALLOWED ON BEACH** Fort Pond Beach **DOGS ALLOWED ON BEACH** Gin Beach **DOGS ALLOWED ON BEACH**
631-668-2461	Hither Hills State Park *NO DOGS ALLOWED IN BATHING AREAS*
631-668-5081	Kirk Park Beach **DOGS ALLOWED ON BEACH**
631-668-2461	Montauk Point State Park *NO DOGS ALLOWED IN BATHING AREAS*
631-669-1000	Shadmoor State Park *NO DOGS ALLOWED IN BATHING AREAS*
631-852-7879	Theodore Roosevelt County Park **LEASHED DOGS ALLOWED ON BEACH**
Orient 631-323-2440	Orient Beach State Park *NO DOGS ALLOWED ON BEACH*
Sag Harbor 631-725-0011	Havens Beach **NO DOGS ALLOWED ON BEACH FROM THE THURSDAY PRECEDING MEMORIAL DAY THROUGH AND INCLUDING THE TUESDAY FOLLOWING LABOR DAY**
Southampton 631-283-0247 631-283-6000	Cooper's Beach **LEASHED DOGS ALLOWED ON BEACH** Flying Point Beach **LEASHED DOGS ALLOWED ON BEACH**
631-852-8205	Meschutt Beach County Park **LEASHED DOGS ALLOWED ON BEACH**
631-283-6011	Ponquoque Beach **DOGS ON BEACH FROM SEPT 15 - MAR 15; NOT WITHIN 50 FEET OF NESTING BIRDS**
631-852-8899	Shinnecock Inlet County Park **LEASHED DOGS ALLOWED ON BEACH**
631-283-6011	Tiana Beach **DOGS ON BEACH FROM SEPT 15 - MAR 15; NOT WITHIN 50 FEET OF NESTING BIRDS**
Southold 631-765-5182	Goose Creek Beach *NO DOGS ALLOWED ON TOWN BEACHES* Kenny's Beach *NO DOGS ALLOWED ON TOWN BEACHES* McCabe's Beach *NO DOGS ALLOWED ON TOWN BEACHES* New Suffolk Beach *NO DOGS ALLOWED ON TOWN BEACHES* Town Beach *NO DOGS ALLOWED ON TOWN BEACHES*

SUFFOLK COUNTY - SOUTH SHORE

Fire Island National Seashore
631-289-4810   **LEASHED DOGS ALLOWED ON LIGHTHOUSE BEACH BUT NOT IN SWIMMING AREAS**

Brookhaven
516-451-6000   Blue Point Beach
NO DOGS ALLOWED ON BEACH

East Islip
631-581-2100   Heckscher State Park
NO DOGS ALLOWED IN BATHING AREAS

Fire Island
631-669-0449
631-852-1313   Robert Moses State Park
DOGS ALLOWED ON FIELD 5
Smith Point County Park
LEASHED DOGS ALLOWED ON BEACH

Patchogue
631-475-4300   Sand Spit Beach
NO DOGS ALLOWED ON BEACH

Westhampton
631-854-4949
631-288-1654   Cupsogue Beach
NO DOGS ALLOWED ON BEACH
Lashley Beach
NO DOGS ALLOWED ON BEACH
Pike's Beach
NO DOGS ALLOWED ON BEACH
Rogers Beach
NO DOGS ALLOWED ON BEACH
Westhampton Beach
NO DOGS ALLOWED ON BEACH

NEW YORK CITY AREA

Brooklyn
718-372-5159   Coney Island
NO DOGS ALLOWED ON THE BEACH

Gateway National Recreation Area
718-318-4300   Fort Tilden
LEASHED DOGS ALLOWED ON BEACH AND BAYSIDE BEACHES
Riis Park
NO DOGS ALLOWED ON BEACH OR BOARDWALK

New Jersey

The summer at the Jersey shore is not a place for dogs but after Labor Day some of America's best white-sand beaches start to open wide for dogs.

Recommended Tail-Friendly Beaches

- **Gateway National Recreation Area.** After Labor Day bring your dog for a long hike on the beach around Sandy Hook with views of the New York skyline.

- **Island Beach State Park.** A rare stretch of ten miles of undeveloped Jersey shoreline is open to your dog year-round.

- **Brigantine Natural Area.** For Atlantic City visitors, go one town north and keep following the ocean until you can go no further. Park and let your dog onto the beach year-round.

- **Corson's Inlet State Park.** Dogs are only allowed September 16 to March 31 but it is worth the wait for this winning combination of hiking trails through the dunes, ocean surf and gentle inlet waters.

- **Higbee Beach.** Hike through the last remaining dune forest on the Delaware Bay to the beach at the tip of Cape May. Your dog is welcome on this bay beach year-round.

Gateway National Recreation Area
732-872-5970   Sandy Hook
DOGS ALLOWED ON BEACH FROM LABOR DAY TO MARCH 15

Asbury Park   Town Beach
732-775-2100   **DOGS ALLOWED IN OFF-SEASON**

Atlantic City   Town Beach
888-228-4748   *NO DOGS ON BEACHES OR BOARDWALK*

Avalon   Town Beach
609-967-3066   **NO DOGS ON BEACH, BOARDWALK OR DUNES BETWEEN MAR 1 AND SEPT 30**

Avon -By-The-Sea 732-502-4510	Town Beach **DOGS ALLOWED ON THE BEACH FROM NOV 1 TO APR 1 BUT NEVER ON BOARDWALK**
Barnegat Light 609-494-9196	Town Beach **DOGS ON BEACHES FROM OCT 1 TO MAY 1**
Beach Haven 609-492-0111	Town Beach *NO DOGS ALLOWED ON BEACH*
Belmar 732-681-3700	Town Beach *NO DOGS ALLOWED ON BEACH*
Bradley Beach 732-776-2999	Town Beach **DOGS ALLOWED FROM OCT 15 TO APR 15**
Brigantine Beach 609-266-5233	Town Beach **DOGS ALLOWED ON BEACH FROM 14TH STREET NORTH TO THE NORTHERNMOST JETTY**
Cape May 609-884-5508	Sunset Beach **DOGS ALLOWED ON BEACH** Town Beach *DOGS ARE NOT ALLOWED ON BEACH, BOARDWALK OR OUTDOOR SHOPPING AREAS*
Cape May Point 609-884-5508	Town Beach *NO DOGS ALLOWED ON BEACH*
Lavallette 732-793-2566	Town Beach *NO DOGS ALLOWED ON BEACH BUT CAN GO ON BOARDWALK FROM AFTER LABOR DAY UNTIL START OF SWIMMING SEASON IN LATE JUNE*
Mantoloking 732-899-6600	Lyman Street Beach **DOGS ALLOWED ON BEACH OCT 1 TO MAY 15** Town Beach **LEASHED DOGS ALLOWED ON BEACH OCT 1 TO MAY 15 ANYTIME AND SUNRISE TO 8 AM AND 6 PM TO SUNSET OTHERWISE**
North Wildwood 609-729-4000	Town Beach **DOGS ON BEACH FROM SEPT 15 TO MAY 15**

Ocean City 609-399-6111	Town Beach **DOGS NEVER ALLOWED ON THE BOARDWALK BUT CAN BE LEASHED ON THE BEACH FROM OCT 1 TO APRIL 30**
Ocean Grove 732-774-1391	Town Beach **DOGS ALLOWED ON BEACH AND BOARDWALK FROM OCT 1 TO MAY 1**
Point Pleasant Beach 732-892-5813	Town Beach **DOGS ALLOWED ON BEACH ANYTIME FROM SEPT 15 TO JUNE 15 AND BEFORE 8 AM AND AFTER 6 PM OTHERWISE**
Sea Isle City 609-263-0050	Town Beach *NO DOGS ALLOWED ON BEACH, BEACH APPROACHES OR PROMENADE AT ANY TIME*
Seaside Park 732-793-0506	Island Beach State Park **DOGS ALLOWED ON NON-RECREATIONAL BEACHES YEAR-ROUND**
Ship Bottom	Town Beach **DOGS ALLOWED ON BEACH AFTER OCT 1**
Spring Lake 732-449-0800	Town Beach **DOGS ALLOWED ON BEACH IN OFF-SEASON**
Stone Harbor	Town Beach **DOGS ALLOWED ON BEACH OCT 1 TO MAR 1**
Strathmere	Town Beach **DOGS ALLOWED ON THE BEACH IN MORNINGS AND EVENINGS IN SEASON**
Surf City	Town Beach *NO DOGS ALLOWED ON BEACH*
Wildwood 609-729-4000	Town Beach *NO DOGS ALLOWED ON BEACH*
Wildwood Crest 609-729-4000	Town Beach *NO DOGS ALLOWED ON BEACH*

Delaware

Off-season, Delaware's sandy ocean beaches are a paradise for dogs. You can even get your dog into the ocean throughout the summer at some beaches. The overlooked beaches along Delaware Bay mean that you can find sand and waves for your dog any time.

Recommended Tail-Friendly Beaches

🐾 **Fowler Beach.** One of the best places in Delaware to bring your dog to the beach. With no development and backed by dunes, this is the Delaware Bay beach that most resembles an ocean beach, the sloping coastline promotes excellent wave action and you can walk your dog for hours.

🐾 **Cape Henlopen State Park.** A long beach that reaches around the cape into the bay. Your dog is welcome throughout the year but can't go on the beach mid-day during the summer.

🐾 **Delaware Seashore State Park.** Stay away from the swimming beaches and you can bring your dog here right through the year. Also access to the gentle waters of Rehoboth Bay where your dog can walk out a half-mile and scarcely get his tummy wet.

DELAWARE BAY

Kitts Hummock	Private
North Bowers	Town Beach **DOGS ALLOWED ANY TIME**
Big Stone Beach	Town Beach **DOGS ALLOWED ANY TIME**
Slaughter Beach	Town Beach **DOGS ALLOWED ANY TIME**
Fowler Beach	Town Beach **DOGS ALLOWED ANY TIME**
Broadkill Beach	Town Beach **DOGS ALLOWED ANY TIME**

ATLANTIC OCEAN

Lewes   Town Beach (Delaware Bay)
**NO DOGS BETWEEN MAY 1 TO
SEPT 30 WHEN OPEN TO SWIMMING**
Cape Henlopen State Park
302-645-8983   **DOGS ALLOWED ON BEACH FROM OCT 1
TO MAY 1**

Rehoboth   Town Beach
302-227-6181   **DOGS ALLOWED ON BEACH AND
BOARDWALK FROM NOV 1 TO APR 1**

Dewey Beach   Town Beach
302-227-6363   **DOGS ARE ALLOWED ON BEACH ALL
YEAR BUT IN SEASON NOT BETWEEN
9:30 AM AND 5:30 PM**

Delaware Seashore State Park
302-227-2800   **DOGS ALLOWED ON BEACH YEAR-
ROUND EXCEPT IN THE SWIMMING
AREAS FROM MAY 1 TO SEPT 30;
ALSO BANNED FROM REHOBOTH BAY
AT TOWER ROAD**

Bethany Beach   Town Beach
302-539-8011   **DOGS ALLOWED ON BEACH AND
BOARDWALK FROM OCT 1 TO APRIL 1**

Fenwick Island   Fenwick Island State Park
302-539-9060   **DOGS ALLOWED ON BEACH FROM OCT 1
TO MAY 1**

*"No one appreciates the very special genius of your
conversation as a dog does."*
-Christopher Morley

Maryland

Sandy beaches on the Chesapeake Bay that welcome dogs are few and far between but once you reach the Atlantic Ocean the sands get friendlier. Stay clear of the Maryland state parks.

Recommended Tail-Friendly Beaches

- **Assateague Island National Seashore.** Miles and miles of undeveloped beach stretch south from the campground. Your dog is always allowed in the Atlantic Ocean here. When you drive onto the island make sure to turn right - straight ahead is the state park that doesn't even allow dogs out of the car.

- **Terrapin Nature Park.** On the Eastern Shore of the Chesapeake Bay, this sandy beach offers splendid views of the Chesapeake-Bay Bridge - the world's longest continuous over-water steel structure. Each year more than twenty million vehicles make the 4.35-mile crossing.

- **Downs Memorial Park.** On the western side of the Chesapeake this county park offers a small sand beach, maybe 40 yards long. But it is secluded, sandy, and it is a dog beach. Your canine swimmer should find these energetic waves to his liking.

ATLANTIC OCEAN

Assateague Island National Seashore
410-641-1441 — **DOGS ALLOWED ON BEACH ANY TIME BUT NOT ON THE TRAILS**

Berlin — Assateague State Park
410-641-2120 — *NO DOGS ALLOWED ON BEACH*

Ocean City — Town Beach
410-250-0125 — **DOGS ALLOWED ON BEACH AND BOARDWALK OCT 1 TO APR 30**

CHESAPEAKE BAY

Annapolis
410-974-2149

Sandy Point State Park
NO DOGS ALLOWED ON BEACH

Chase
410-592-2897

Gunpowder Falls State Park-Hammerman
NO DOGS ALLOWED ON BEACH

Chesapeake Beach
410-257-2230
410-535-1600 x225

Bayfront Park
DOGS ALLOWED ON BEACH
Breezy Point Public Beach
DOGS ALLOWED ON BEACH

Dameron
301-475-4572

Elms Public Beach
DOGS ALLOWED ON BEACH

Edgemere
410-592-2897

North Point State Park
DOGS ALLOWED ON SMALL BEACH

Essex
410-887-3780

Rocky Point Park
NO DOGS ALLOWED ON BEACH

Lusby
800-784-5380
410-586-1477

Calvert Cliffs State Park
NO DOGS ALLOWED ON BEACH
Flag Ponds Nature Park
DOGS ALLOWED ON BEACH

Matapeake

Matapeake Park
DOGS ALLOWED UNLEASHED ON BEACH

North Beach
410-257-9610

North Beach Public Beach
NO DOGS ALLOWED ON BEACH

Pinehurst
410-222-6230

Downs Memorial Park
DOG BEACH IN PARK

Scotland
301-872-5688

Point Lookout State Park
DOGS ALLOWED ON BEACH NORTH OF CAUSEWAY

Stevensville
410-758-0835

Terrapin Nature Park
DOGS ALLOWED ON BEACH

Doggin The Chesapeake

The Chesapeake Bay is one of our great recreation destinations (***www. baygateways.net***). More than 1 in every 15 Americans live within a short drive of the nation's largest estuary and millions come each year for the sailing, the lighthouses, the Atlantic Blue Crabs... What about for your dog? Some of the best Maryland state parks on the Bay don't allow dogs (Calvert Cliffs, Sandy Point) but there are some fine beaches to take your dog to nonetheless. Here are the 13 best -

1. **FIRST LANDING STATE PARK** (*Virginia, south mouth of Bay*). One of the finest state parks you'll find anywhere features an ocean-type beach at the mouth of the Chesapeake. You can easily hike with your dog for over an hour on the beach with views of the Chesapeake Bay Bridge Tunnel and ocean-going vessels in view the entire time.

2. **HUGHLETT POINT NATURAL AREA** (*Virginia, western shore*). You will start your exploration with your dog here on a wide, soft and exceedingly agreeable path through a fragrant loblolly forest. Soon you will pop out on the beach of the Chesapeake Bay where you will be excused for thinking you have just landed on Tom Hanks' deserted island in *Cast Away*. Ghost trees and fallen trunks pepper the enchanted shore - ineffective guardians against the relentless Chesapeake wave action.

3. **KIPTOPEKE STATE PARK** (*Virginia, eastern shore*). Features more than a half-mile of wide sandy beaches, backed by dunes. Off-shore nine concrete World War II surplus ships have been sunk as a breakwater, leaving gentle waves for your dog to play in. Also an easy 1.5-mile *Baywoods Trail* when you want to take a break from the water. Dogs are welcome in the campground.

4. **TERRAPIN NATURE PARK** (*Maryland, eastern shore at Bay Bridge*). Terrapin Park has over 4,000 feet of beach frontage at the tip of Kent Island. Firsky waves and canine swimming in the north shadow of the Bay Bridge. The trail to the beach takes you across oyster chaff.

5. **DOWNS MEMORIAL PARK** (*Maryland, western shore north of Annapolis*). Looking for a dog-friendly park? At Downs Memorial Park there is a "pet parking" stall outside the information center. A dog drinking bowl is chained to a human water fountain. Best of all is *Dog Beach*, an isolated, scruffy 40-yard stretch of sand where you can let the dog off leash for canine aquatics in the Chesapeake Bay. The wave action is just right for dogs and there is enough sand for digging. Need we say more?

6. **FLAG PONDS NATURE PARK** (*Maryland, western shore - Lusby*). Thick woods and an isolated sandy beach backed by wild grasses but don't come too early - the park doesn't open until 9:00 a.m and is only open Memorial Day to Labor Day and weekends all year round.

7. **MATAPEAKE PARK** (*Maryland, eastern shore, south of Bay Bridge*). This small park on the Chesapeake Bay features a pleasant one-mile wood-chip trail through a pine forest but the reason to come here is a stretch of sandy beach where your dog is welcome off-leash. The beach is a bit too industrial for sunbathers which makes it the perfect place for dogs to romp. Matapeake Park is just south of the Bay Bridge with splendid views of the bay and bridge.

8. **GLOUCESTER POINT PARK** (*Virginia, western shore, at the mouth of the York River*). Here in the shadow of America's longest double-swing bridge your dog will find a smooth sand beach and swimming in the light waves of the bay. There is also a small grassy area to roll around in.

9. **WYE ISLAND NATURAL RESOURCES MANAGEMENT AREA** (*Maryland, eastern shore*). The *Ferry Landing Trail* was once the only access road to the island, lined with Osage orange trees imported to serve as a natural fence. Osage orange trees originated in a small region of Texas, Oklahoma and Arkansas, which was home to the Osage Indians, who used its wood for bows. This mile-long path ends at a small, sandy beach.

10.   **POINT LOOKOUT STATE PARK** (*Maryland, southern tip of western shore*). A Civil War prison to hold Confederate soldiers was built here at the mouth of the Potomac River and is the main attraction of the park but dogs aren't allowed here. Before crossing the causeway to the island, however, is a small, sandy dog beach with excellent wave action.

11.   **EASTERN NECK NATIONAL WILDLIFE REFUGE** (*Maryland, eastern shore, south of Rock Hall*). Technically the secluded sandy beach at the end of the Boxes Point Trail is on the Chester River but your don't won't quibble when she tests these fun waves.

12.   **ELK NECK STATE PARK** (*Maryland, eastern shore, 11 miles west of Northeast*). The park is situated on 100-foot bluffs above the Chesapeake Bay where the Elk and Northeast rivers converge. Narrow, informal trails lead down to the water's edge where gaps in the stone breakwater produce little sandy beaches just for your dog.

13.   **NORTH POINT STATE PARK** (*Maryland, western shore, east of Baltimore*). Although only 20 acres in size, the Bay Shore Park was considered one of the finest amusement parks ever built along the Chesapeake Bay. Opened in 1906, the park featured an Edwardian-style dance hall, bowling alley and restaurant set in among gardens and curving pathways. There were rides such as a water toboggan and Sea Swing. Visitors would travel to the shore from Baltimore on a trolley line. Your dog can explore the remains and dive in the Chesapeake at a small wading beach at the Visitor Center.

Virginia

Virginia make splenty of allowances for dogs on its beaches, even at its popular sand and surf spots.

Recommended Tail-Friendly Beaches

🐾 **Virginia Beach.** You can get your dog on all of Virginia Beach's clean, white sand at some point during the year; after Halloween every grain is open to dogs from Cape Henry to the North Carolina border.

🐾 **First Landing State Park.** In the summer, while you wait for Virginia Beach around the corner to open for your dog, you can come to the wide sand beach at the mouth of the Chesapeake Bay. Just move your dog down away from the bathhouse.

ATLANTIC OCEAN

Chincoteague 757-336-6122	National Wildlife Refuge *NO DOGS ALLOWED IN REFUGE BUT CAN GO LEASHED ON BEACH IN NATIONAL SEASHORE*
Virginia Beach 757-721-2412	Back Bay National Wildlife Refuge **DOGS ALLOWED ON BEACH OCT 1 TO MAR 31**
757-426-7128	False Cape State Park **DOGS ALLOWED BY BOAT OR BEACH TRAIL NOV TO MAR; BOAT ONLY APR TO SEPT AND NOT IN SWIMMING AREAS**
757-426-7200	Little Island Park (Sandbridge) **DOGS ALLOWED ON BEACH BUT NOT IN SWIMMING AREAS**
800-822-3224	North End-41st to 80th Street **DOGS ALLOWED ON BEACH THE DAY AFTER LABOR DAY TO THE FRIDAY BEFORE MEMORIAL DAY; IN SUMMER DOGS ALLOWED ON RESIDENTIAL BEACHES ABOVE 42ND STREET BEFORE 10 AM AND AFTER 6 PM** Oceanfront-1st to 40th Street("The Strip") **DOGS ALLOWED ON BEACH THE DAY AFTER LABOR DAY TO THE FRIDAY BEFORE MEMORIAL DAY**

CHESAPEAKE BAY

| Cape Charles | Kiptopeke State Park |
| 757-331-2267 | **LEASHED DOGS ALLOWED ON BEACH** |

| Gloucester Point | Gloucester Point Beach |
| 804-642-9474 | **LEASHED DOGS ALLOWED ON BEACH IN PARK** |

| Kilmarnock | Hughlett Point Natural Area |
| | **DOGS ALLOWED ON BEACH** |

| Mathews | Bethel Beach |
| 804-725-4BAY | *NO DOGS ALLOWED ON BEACH* |

| Virginia Beach | First Landing State Park |
| 757-412-2300 | **LEASHED DOGS ALLOWED ON BEACH** |

"I can't think of anything that brings me closer to tears than when my old dog - completely exhausted afters a hard day in the field - limps away from her nice spot in front of the fire and comes over to where I'm sitting and puts her head in my lap, a paw over my knee, and closes her eyes, and goes back to sleep. I don't know what I've done to deserve that kind of friend."
-Gene Hill

North Carolina

By any definition, the public beaches of the barrier islands of North Carolina are among the dog-friendliest in North America.

Recommended Tail-Friendly Beaches

🐾 **Duck.** This beach town in the northern Outer Banks allows dogs on the beach year-round under voice control. If it's a long walk you are after, head north.

🐾 **Cape Hatteras National Seashore.** If it is really a long walk you are after, there are some 70 miles of dog-friendly sand here. Ocracoke Island, reached via a free ferry, delivers an undeveloped, dune-backed stretch of sand that is second to none for dogs.

🐾 **Emerald Isle.** Most towns on Crystal Coast permit dogs on the beach year-round; Emerald Isle has the most parking.

🐾 **Fort Fisher Recreation Area.** Just avoid the swimming areas and you have miles of wide, white sand beaches open to your dog year-round.

🐾 **Sunset Beach.** Dogs are allowed year-round after 6:00 p.m. to soak in that sunset, walking south. Parking can be a problem at this residential beach.

OUTER BANKS

Cape Hatteras National Seashore
252-473-2111   **DOGS ALLOWED ON BEACH YEAR-ROUND ON 6-FOOT LEASH**

Corolla   Town Beach
877-CURRITUCK   **DOGS ALLOWED ON BEACH UNDER VOICE CONTROL**

Duck   Town Beach
252-255-1234   **UNLEASHED DOGS ALLOWED ON BEACH**

Kill Devil Hills Town Beach
252-449-5300   **DOGS ALLOWED ON BEACH FROM MID-SEPT TO MID-MAY**

Kitty Hawk
252-261-3552

Town Beach
**DOGS ALLOWED UNLEASHED SEPT 1 TO
JUN 1 AND BEFORE 10 AM AND AFTER
6 PM; OTHERWISE, LEASHED DOGS
ALLOWED ON BEACH 10 AM TO 6 PM
JUN 1 TO SEPT 1**

Nags Head
252-441-5508

Town Beach
**DOGS ALLOWED ON BEACH YEAR
ROUND ON 10-FOOT LEASH**

Southern Shores

Town Beach
**DOGS ALLOWED ON BEACH SEPT 15 TO
MAY 15**

CRYSTAL COAST

Cape Lookout National Seashore
252-728-2250

**DOGS ALLOWED ON BEACH YEAR-
ROUND ON 6-FOOT LEASH**

Atlantic Beach
252-726-3775

Fort Macon
**DOGS ALLOWED ON THE
NON-SWIMMING BEACH**

252-726-2121

Town Beach
**LEASHED DOGS ALLOWED ON BEACH
EXCEPT IN THE CIRCLE AND BEACH
AREA IN FRONT OF CIRCLE FROM
EASTER TO LABOR DAY**

Pine Knolls
252-247-4353

Town Beach
**DOGS ALLOWED ON BEACH ANYTIME
WITH A 16-FOOT MAXIMUM LEASH**

Salter Path

Town Beach
DOGS ALLOWED ON LEASH ANYTIME

Indian Beach

Town Beach
DOGS ALLOWED ON BEACH

Emerald Isle
252-354-3424

Town Beach
**LEASHED DOGS ALLOWED ON BEACH
ANYTIME**

Swansboro
910-326-4881

Hammocks Beach State Park
**LEASHED DOGS ARE ALLOWED ON
ANY BEACH THAT IS NOT A SWIMMING
BEACH**

CAPE FEAR

Topsail Beach
910-328-5841

Town Beach
LEASHED DOGS ALLOWED MAY 15 THROUGH SEPT 30 AND UNDER VOICE CONTROL AT OTHER TIMES

Wrightsville
910-256-7910

Town Beach
LEASHED DOGS ALLOWED ON BEACH FROM OCT 1 TO APR 1

Carolina Beach
910-458-8434

Town Beach
NO DOGS ALLOWED ON BEACH MAR 1 TO OCT 31

Kure Beach
910-458-4798

Fort Fisher Recreation Area
LEASHED DOGS ALLOWED ON BEACH IN ANY NON-SWIMMING AREA
Town Beach

910-458-5798

NO DOGS ALLOWED ON BEACH APRIL TO SEPTEMBER

BRUNSWICK ISLANDS

Caswell Beach
910-278-5471

Town Beach
LEASHED DOGS ALLOWED ON BEACH

Oak Island
910-278-5011

Town Beach
LEASHED DOGS ALLOWED ON BEACH

Holden Beach
910-842-6488

Town Beach
LEASHED DOGS ALLOWED ON BEACH LABOR DAY TO MEMORIAL DAY AND DURING THE SUMMER BEFORE 9:00 A.M. AND AFTER 5:00 P.M.

Ocean Isle Beach
910-579-2166

Town Beach
LEASHED DOGS ALLOWED ON BEACH LABOR DAY TO MEMORIAL DAY AND DURING THE SUMMER BEFORE 9:00 A.M. AND AFTER 6:00 P.M.

Sunset Beach
910-579-6297

Town Beach
LEASHED DOGS ALLOWED ON BEACH LABOR DAY TO MEMORIAL DAY AND DURING THE SUMMER BEFORE 8:00 A.M. AND AFTER 6:00 P.M.

South Carolina

Get away from the people and commercial beaches and there is plenty of dog-friendly sand in the Palmetto state. The state parks at the South Carolina coast should be your first choice - welcoming to dogs with plenty of parking for your admission fee.

Recommended Tail-Friendly Beaches

- **Hunting Island Beach State Park.** The palmetto trees come right down the beach in this marvelous park. You won't wonder why the jungle scenes from *Forrest Gump* were filmed here.

- **Edisto Beach State Park.** Plenty of room for your dog to stretch out on the sand here but if you run out of beach you can keep hiking on the dog-friendly residential beach next door.

- **Myrtle Beach State Park.** Dogs aren't allowed on the beach at the popular resort in the summer so just mosey three miles south and enjoy this undeveloped beachfront with your dog. Over a mile of dune-backed sand in the park alone.

- **Huntington Beach State Park.** Some of the money from the original Transcontinental Railroad dribbled down to the magnificent surfside estate built here in the early 20th century. Today, head for the northern section of the park for long walks on the beach and in the maritime forest.

North Myrtle Beach 843-280-5570	Town Beach **DOGS ALLOWED ON BEACH SEPT 15 TO MAY 15 ANYTIME; OTHERWISE BEFORE 9 AM AND AFTER 5 PM**
Myrtle Beach 800-356-3016	21st Avenue N to 13th Avenue S *NO DOGS ALLOWED ON BEACH* Rest of Town Beach **DOGS ALLOWED ON BEACH SEPT 15 TO MAY 15 ANYTIME; OTHERWISE BEFORE 9 AM AND AFTER 5 PM**
Surfside Beach 843-913-6111	Town Beach **DOGS ALLOWED ON BEACH SEPT 16 TO MAY 14**

Garden City Beach
843-546-8436

Town Beach
DOGS ALLOWED ON BEACH UNDER VOICE COMMAND

South Myrtle Beach
843-238-4325

Myrtle Beach State Park
LEASHED DOGS ALLOWED ON BEACH

Murrells Inlet
843-237-4440

Huntington Beach State Park
LEASHED DOGS ALLOWED ON BEACH

Litchfield Beach
843-546-8436

Town Beach
DOGS ALLOWED ON BEACH UNDER VOICE CONTROL

Pawleys Island
843-237-1698

Town Beach
LEASHED DOGS ALLOWED ON BEACH MAY TO OCT; UNDER VOICE CONTROL OTHER TIMES

Georgetown
843-546-8436

Town Beach
DOGS ALLOWED ON BEACH

Isle of Palms
843-886-3863

Town Beach
DOGS ALLOWED ON BEACH UNDER VOICE CONTROL FROM 5 AM TO 8 AM WITH OWNER HOLDING LEASH; LEASHED DOGS ALLOWED ON BEACH OTHER HOURS

Sullivans Island
843-958-4000

Town Beach
NO DOGS 10 AM TO 6 PM APR 1 TO OCT 31; ALLOWED OFF-LEASH BEFORE 10 AM AND ON LEASH AFTER 6 PM; FROM NOV 1 TO MAR 31 ARE ALLOWED OFF-LEASH FROM 5 AM TO NOON

Charleston
843-588-2426

Folly Beach
DOGS ALLOWED ON BEACH IN EVENING IN SUMMER AND ENTIRE DAY OTHERWISE

Kiawah Island
843-768-2395

Town Beach
LEASHED DOGS ALLOWED FROM MAR 15 TO OCT 31 AND UNDER VOICE CONTROL REST OF YEAR

Edisto Beach 843-869-2756	Edisto Beach State Park **LEASHED DOGS ALLOWED ON BEACH** Town Beach **LEASHED DOGS ALLOWED ON BEACH**
Beaufort 843-838-2011	Hunting Island State Park **LEASHED DOGS ALLOWED ON BEACH**
Hilton Head Island 843-785-3673	Driessden's Beach **LEASHED DOGS ALLOWED ON BEACH** Folly Field Beach **LEASHED DOGS ALLOWED ON BEACH**

"We are alone, absolutely alone on this chance planet;
and, amid all the forms of life that surround us, not one,
excepting the dog, has made an alliance with us."
-Maurice Maeterlinck

Georgia

The beaches on Georgia's barrier islands are mostly under control of resorts and the Golden Isles are most welcoming to dogs. Savannah's beach at Tybee Island is closed to dogs.

<u>Cumberland Island National Seashore</u>
818-817-3421   **LEASHED DOGS ALLOWED ON BEACH BUT CAN BE REACHED BY PRIVATE BOAT ONLY**

Jekyll Island   Oceanfront Beach
912-635-3636   **NO DOGS ALLOWED ON BEACH IN SEASON FROM 9 AM TO 4:30 PM; OTHERWISE LEASHED DOGS ALLOWED**

Sea Island   Oceanfront Beach
912-265-0620   **NO DOGS ALLOWED ON BEACH IN SEASON FROM 9 AM TO 4:30 PM; OTHERWISE LEASHED DOGS ALLOWED**

St. Simons Island   Oceanfront Beach
800-933-2627   **NO DOGS ALLOWED ON BEACH IN SEASON FROM 9 AM TO 4:30 PM; OTHERWISE LEASHED DOGS ALLOWED**

Tybee Island   Town Beach
800-868-2322   *NO DOGS ALLOWED ON BEACH*

"Any man who does not like dogs and want them does not deserve to be in the White House."
-Calvin Coolidge

Florida

Florida ranks among the most dog-unfriendly of states. Entire counties and regions ban dogs from the beach. There are so many prohibitions already against dogs on Florida beaches that when they change, it is typically in favor of dogs. For the Atlantic beaches the northeast part of the state around Jacksonville offers some of the best beaches for dogs in the state but heading south, below Daytona dogs are almost universally banned from the sand.

Recommended Tail-Friendly Beaches

- **Amelia Island.** If you are driving south into Florida you will want to get your dog onto the sand as soon as possible. This residential/vacation beach will fill the bill nicely. It will get dreary for dogs along the Atlantic Ocean soon enough.

- **Sombrero Beach.** Sombrero Beach in the Florida Keys is actually a park with a playground planted in the white sand, picnic tables and patches of groomed grass. Admission is free and your dog is welcome on the beach and in the water. The wide beach is framed by palm trees whose only downside is that they don't drop any branches for your dog to fetch in the clear emerald waters. The soft sands extend far into the water so you can join your dog in the gentle surf.

- **Fort DeSoto Park.** Fort DeSoto was named "America's Best Beach" by Dr. Beach in 2005. Your dog can't actually go on that champion Gulf of Mexico beach but around the corner there is an enormous dog park and paw-friendly groomed sand on Tampa Bay. There are even doggie showers to spruce up a bit before you head home.

- **Bonita Beach.** A short walk through the trees leads to a long beach and shallow, gentle water on the Gulf of Mexico - and it is just for dogs.

- **St. Andrews Beach.** Another award-winning beach your dog can't enjoy. But when you pull into the park, turn left when everyone else goes straight for the beach parking lot. Your destination is the mostly ignored Grand Lagoon side of the park you and your dog can enjoy a narrow strip of sand and leisurely swimming in the shallow, gentle waters. The Grand Lagoon is reached by the *Heron Pond Trail*, a rolling exploration of the scrubby dunes.

FIRST COAST

Amelia Island	Burney Beach Park
904-277-1221	**LEASHED DOGS ALLOWED ON BEACH**
904-321-5700	Fernadina Beach
	LEASHED DOGS ALLOWED ON BEACH
904-277-7274	Fort Clinch State Park
	NO DOGS ALLOWED ON BEACH
904-277-1221	Peter's Point Beach
	LEASHED DOGS ALLOWED ON BEACH
	Scott Road Beach
	LEASHED DOGS ALLOWED ON BEACH
Jacksonville Area	Atlantic Beach
904-798-9111 x10	**LEASHED DOGS ALLOWED ON BEACH**
904-251-2320	Big Talbot Island State Park
	NO DOGS ALLOWED ON BEACH
	Fort George State Cultural Site
	NO DOGS ALLOWED ON BEACH
904-251-3335	Huguenot Memorial Park
	DOGS ALLOWED ON BEACH
904-798-9111 x10	Jacksonville Beach
	DOGS ALLOWED ON BEACH EXCEPT 8 AM TO 5 PM FROM NOV TO MAR AND 9 AM TO 7 PM APR TO OCT
904-249-4700	Kathryn Abbey Hanna Park
	DOGS ALLOWED ON BEACH
904-251-2320	Little Talbot Island State Park
	NO DOGS ALLOWED ON BEACH
904-798-9111 x10	Neptune Beach
	DOGS ALLOWED ON BEACH BEFORE 9 AM AND AFTER 5 PM
	North Beach
	NO DOGS ALLOWED ON BEACH
	Ponte Vedra Beach
	DOGS ALLOWED ON BEACH UP TO HIGHWATER LINE
	South Ponte Vedra Beach
	DOGS ALLOWED ON BEACH UP TO HIGHWATER LINE
	Vilano Beach
	DOGS ALLOWED ON BEACH

St. Augustine Area	Anastasia State Park
904-825-1007	*NO DOGS ALLOWED ON BEACH*
904-439-6888	Beverly Beach
	DOGS ALLOWED ON BEACH
904-825-1007	Crescent Beach
	LEASHED DOGS ALLOWED ON BEACH
904-424-2100	New Smyrna Beach
	DOGS ALLOWED ON THE BEACH IN DESIGNATED AREAS
904-825-1007	St. Augustine Beach
	LEASHED DOGS ALLOWED ON BEACH

SPACE COAST

Cape Canaveral National Seashore

| 321-267-1110 | *NO DOGS ALLOWED ON BEACH OR BEYOND PARKING LOT* |

Daytona Area	Dahlia Park
386-322-5000	*NO DOGS ALLOWED ON BEACH*
386-947-3010	Daytona Beach
	NO DOGS ALLOWED ON BEACH
386-517-2000	Flagler Beach
	DOGS ALLOWED ON BEACH BETWEEN 10TH STREET N AND 10TH STREET S
386-517-2086	Gamble Rogers Memorial State Park
	NO DOGS ALLOWED ON BEACH
396-424-2935	Smyrna Dune Park
	DOGS ALLOWED ON BEACH BUT MUST BE LEASHED AT ALL TIMES, INCLUDING IN THE WATER
386-322-3000	South Daytona Beach
	NO DOGS ALLOWED ON BEACH
386-677-0311	Tomoka State Park
	NO DOGS ALLOWED ON BEACH

Melbourne Area	Cocoa Beach
321-868-3333	*NO DOGS ALLOWED ON BEACH*
800-872-1969	Indialantic Beach
	NO DOGS ALLOWED ON BEACH
321-724-5860	Melbourne Beach
	NO DOGS ALLOWED ON THE BEACH
321-773-4407	Satellite Beach
	NO DOGS ALLOWED ON BEACH BUT A DOG PARK IS IN TOWN NEAR LIBRARY
321-984-4852	Sebastian Inlet State Park
	NO DOGS ALLOWED ON OCEAN BEACH BUT DOGS ALLOWED ON INLET SIDE

Sebastian Area
772-589-9223

Ambler Sands Beach
NO DOGS ALLOWED ON BEACH
Golden Sands Beach
NO DOGS ALLOWED ON BEACH
Sea Grape Trail Beach
NO DOGS ALLOWED ON BEACH
Treasure Shores Park
NO DOGS ALLOWED ON BEACH
Turtle Trail Beach
NO DOGS ALLOWED ON BEACH
Wabes Beach Park
NO DOGS ALLOWED ON BEACH

TREASURE COAST

Fort Pierce
561-468-3985

Fort Pierce Inlet State Park
*NO DOGS ALLOWED ON OCEAN BEACH BUT
DOGS ALLOWED ON INLET SIDE*
Pepper Beach State Park
NO DOGS ALLOWED ON BEACH

Highland Beach
561-278-4540

Town Beach
LEASHED DOGS ALLOWED ON BEACH

Hutchinson Island
732-334-3444

Alex's Beach
NO DOGS ALLOWED ON BEACH
Bathtub Reef Park
NO DOGS ALLOWED ON BEACH
Bob Graham Beach
NO DOGS ALLOWED ON BEACH
Chastain Beach
NO DOGS ALLOWED ON BEACH
Fletcher Beach
NO DOGS ALLOWED ON BEACH

Hutchinson Area
732-334-3444

Glasscock Beach
NO DOGS ALLOWED ON BEACH
Sea Turtle/Jensen Beach Park
NO DOGS ALLOWED ON BEACH
Stuart Beach
NO DOGS ALLOWED ON BEACH
Tiger Shores Beach
NO DOGS ALLOWED ON BEACH
Virginia Forrest Beach
NO DOGS ALLOWED ON BEACH
Waveland Beach
NO DOGS ALLOWED ON BEACH

Juno Beach 561-626-4122	Juno Beach *NO DOGS ALLOWED ON BEACH* Loggerhead Park *NO DOGS ALLOWED ON BEACH* Ocean Cay Park *NO DOGS ALLOWED ON BEACH*
Jupiter 561-546-6141 561-746-5134	Hobe Sound National Wildlife Refuge **DOGS ALLOWED ON BEACH** Carlin Park **DOGS ALLOWED ON BEACH UNDER VOICE CONTROL IN NON-GUARDED AREAS** Dubois Park **DOGS ALLOWED ON BEACH UNDER VOICE CONTROL IN NON-GUARDED AREAS** Jupiter Beach **DOGS ALLOWED ON BEACH UNDER VOICE CONTROL IN NON-GUARDED AREAS**
Orchid 561-567-3491	Town Beach *NO DOGS ALLOWED ON BEACH*
Tequesta 561-746-7111	Coral Cove Beach *NO DOGS ALLOWED ON BEACH*
Vero Beach 561-567-3491	Town Beach **DOGS ALLOWED ON UNPROTECTED BEACHES**

GOLD COAST

Boca Raton 561-393-7806 561-966-6600 561-393-7806	Red Reef Park *NO DOGS ALLOWED ON BEACH* South Beach Park *NO DOGS ALLOWED ON BEACH* South Inlet Park *NO DOGS ALLOWED ON BEACH* Spanish Reef Park *NO DOGS ALLOWED ON BEACH*
Boynton Beach 561-375-6226 561-966-6600	Boynton Public Beach *NO DOGS ALLOWED ON BEACH* Gulf Stream County Park *NO DOGS ALLOWED ON BEACH*
Dania 954-923-2833	John U. Lloyd Beach State Park *NO DOGS ALLOWED ON BEACH*

Delray Beach 561-243-7250	Anchor Park *NO DOGS ALLOWED ON BEACH* Atlantic Dunes Park Beach *NO DOGS ALLOWED ON BEACH* Delray Municipal **DOGS ALLOWED ON SIDEWALK AND GRASSY AREA WEST OF THE DUNE LINE ON THE EAST SIDE OF A-1A** Sandoway Park *NO DOGS ALLOWED ON BEACH*
Fort Lauderdale 954-761-5346 954-828-7275	D.C. Alexander Park *NO DOGS ALLOWED ON BEACH* Fort Lauderdale Dog Beach **100-YARD STRIP OF BEACH AT SUNRISE AND A1A ON SATURDAYS AND SUNDAYS FROM 3-6 PM; ONE DAY PASS AND SUNDAYS FROM 3-6 PM; ONE DAY PASS REQUIRED** Fort Lauderdale Beach-North *NO DOGS ALLOWED ON BEACH* Fort Lauderdale Beach-South *NO DOGS ALLOWED ON BEACH*
954-761-5346	Harbor Beach *NO DOGS ALLOWED ON BEACH*
954-564-4521	Hugh Taylor Birch State Park *NO DOGS ALLOWED ON BEACH BUT CAN GO IN PARK*
954-761-5346	Vista Park *NO DOGS ALLOWED ON BEACH*
Hallandale 954-457-1456	Hallandale Beach *NO DOGS ALLOWED ON BEACH*
Hillsboro Inlet 954-480-4429 954-776-0576	Deerfield Beach *NO DOGS ALLOWED ON BEACH* Friedt Park *NO DOGS ALLOWED ON BEACH* Hillsboro Beach *NO DOGS ALLOWED ON BEACH* Lauderdale-by-the-Sea Beach *NO DOGS ALLOWED ON BEACH*
954-786-4111	North Ocean Park *NO DOGS ALLOWED ON BEACH*
954-941-2940	Pompano Beach Public Beach *NO DOGS ALLOWED ON BEACH*
Hollywood 954-921-3423	Hollywood Public Beach *NO DOGS ALLOWED ON BEACH* North Hollywood Beach *NO DOGS ALLOWED ON BEACH*

Homestead 305-230-7275	Biscayne National Park *LEASHED DOGS ALLOWED AT CONVOY MAINLAND AND IN DEVELOPED AREAS OF ELLIOTT KEY BUT NO BEACHES OR OTHER ISLANDS*
Key Biscayne 305-361-5811 305-361-7385	Bill Baggs Cape Florida State Park *NO DOGS ALLOWED ON BEACH* Crandon Park Beach *NO DOGS ALLOWED ON BEACH*
Lake Worth Area 561-533-7367 561-540-5735 561-233-3000 561-533-7367	Lake Worth Beach *NO DOGS ALLOWED ON BEACH* Lantana Municipal Beach Park *NO DOGS ALLOWED ON BEACH* Manalapan Beach *NO DOGS ALLOWED ON BEACH* Phipps Ocean Park *NO DOGS ALLOWED ON BEACH* Richard G. Kreusler Park *NO DOGS ALLOWED ON BEACH*
Miami 305-250-5360	Rickenbacker Causeway and Beach **ALLOWED ON BEACH HERE AND NOWHERE ELSE IN MIAMI**
Miami Beach 305-866-4633 305-673-7400 305-884-1101 305-944-3040 305-673-7400	Bal Harbor Beach *NO DOGS ALLOWED ON BEACH* Collins Park *NO DOGS ALLOWED ON BEACH* Golden Beach *NO DOGS ALLOWED ON BEACH* Haulover Beach *NO DOGS ALLOWED ON BEACH* Indian Beach Park *NO DOGS ALLOWED ON BEACH* Lummus Park *NO DOGS ALLOWED ON BEACH* North Shore Park *NO DOGS ALLOWED ON BEACH* Oleta River State Park *NO DOGS ALLOWED ON BEACH* South Beach *NO DOGS ALLOWED ON BEACH* South Pointe Park *NO DOGS ALLOWED ON BEACH*
Singer Island 561-624-6950	John D. MacArthur Beach State Park *NO DOGS ALLOWED ON BEACH*
South Miami 305-665-5475	Matheson Hammock County Park *NO DOGS ALLOWED ON BEACH*

THE KEYS

Bahia Key
305-872-2353

Bahia Honda State Park
NO DOGS ALLOWED ON BEACH
Little Duck Key County Park
DOGS ALLOWED ON BEACH

Key Largo
305-451-1202

John Pennekamp Coral Reef State Park
NO DOGS ALLOWED ON BEACH

Key West
305-292-8227

Clarence Higgs Memorial Beach
NO DOGS ALLOWED ON BEACH
Dog Beach
**DOGS ALLOWED ON SLIM BEACH AT
WADDELL & VERNON AVENUES**

305-292-6713

Fort Zachary Taylor Historic State Park
NO DOGS ALLOWED ON BEACH OR FORT

305-292-8227

Smathers Beach
NO DOGS ALLOWED ON BEACH

Long Key
305-664-4815

Long Key State Park
NO DOGS ALLOWED ON BEACH

Lower Matecumbe
305-292-4560

Anne's Beach
DOGS ALLOWED ON BEACH

Marathon
305-292-4560

Sombrero Beach
DOGS ALLOWED ON BEACH

Tavernier
305-852-7161

Harry Harris Park
*NO DOGS ON BEACH IN SWIMMING
AREAS*

Your Dog On The
Gulf Of Mexico
Beaches...

SUNCOAST

Fort Myers Area	Algiers Beach
941-472-1080	**DOGS ALLOWED ON SANIBEL ISLAND BEACHES**
239-992-5011	Bonita Beach
	DOGS ALLOWED AT BONITA DOG BEACH
941-472-1080	Bowman's Beach
	DOGS ALLOWED ON SANIBEL ISLAND BEACHES
941-472-1080	Captiva Beach
	NO DOGS ALLOWED ON CAPTIVA ISLAND BEACHES
941-964-0375	Cayo Costa State Park
	NO DOGS ALLOWED ON BEACH
239-463-4588	Fort Myers Beach Park
	NO DOGS ALLOWED ON BEACH
941-964-0375	Gasparilla Island State Park
	NO DOGS ALLOWED ON BEACH
941-472-1080	Lighthouse Pier and Park
	DOGS ALLOWED ON SANIBEL ISLAND BEACHES
239-463-4588	Lovers Key Carl E. Johnson State Park
	NO DOGS ALLOWED ON BEACH
239-992-5011	New Pass Beach
	DOGS ALLOWED ON BEACH
941-472-1080	Sanibel Beach
	DOGS ALLOWED ON SANIBEL ISLAND BEACHES
	Turner Beach
	NO DOGS ALLOWED ON CAPTIVA ISLAND BEACHES
Naples Area	Barefoot Beach State Park
239-597-6196	*NO DOGS ALLOWED ON BEACH*
	Delnor-Wiggins Pass State Park
	NO DOGS ALLOWED ON BEACH
239-213-1015	Clam Pass Beach
	NO DOGS ALLOWED ON BEACH
	Lely Barefoot Beach
	NO DOGS ALLOWED ON BEACH
239-434-4698	Lowdermilk Park Beach
	NO DOGS ALLOWED ON BEACH
	Naples Municipal Beach
239-213-1015	*NO DOGS ALLOWED ON BEACH*
	South Marco Beach
	NO DOGS ALLOWED ON BEACH
239-389-5000	Tigertail Beach
	NO DOGS ALLOWED ON BEACH
239-597-6196	Vanderbilt Beach
	NO DOGS ALLOWED ON BEACH

Sarasota Area	Bayfront Park
941-742-5923	*NO DOGS ALLOWED ON BEACH*
941-627-1628	Blind Pass Beach
	NO DOGS ALLOWED ON BEACH
941-742-5923	Bradenton Beach
	NO DOGS ALLOWED ON BEACH
941-488-2236	Brohard Park Beach
	DOGS ALLOWED ON BEACH UNDER VOICE CONTROL BEHIND WASTE WATER PLANT
941-627-1628	Chadwick Park at Englewood Beach
	NO DOGS ALLOWED ON THE BEACH
941-742-5926	Coquina Beach
	NO DOGS ALLOWED ON BEACH
	Cortez Beach
	NO DOGS ALLOWED ON BEACH
941-964-0375	Don Pedro Island State Park
	NO DOGS ALLOWED ON BEACH
941-627-1628	Englewood Beach
	NO DOGS ALLOWED ON BEACH
941-742-5923	Greek Island
	NO DOGS ALLOWED ON BEACH
	Holmes Beach
	NO DOGS ALLOWED ON BEACH
941-861-5000	Lido Beach
	NO DOGS ALLOWED ON BEACH
941-627-1628	Manasota Beach
	NO DOGS ALLOWED ON BEACH
941-742-5923	Manatee County Beach
	NO DOGS ALLOWED ON BEACH
941-861-5000	Nokomis Beach
	NO DOGS ALLOWED ON BEACH
	North Jetty Park
	NO DOGS ALLOWED ON BEACH
	Palmer Point South
	NO DOGS ALLOWED ON BEACH
941-627-1628	Port Charlotte Beach Park
	NO DOGS ALLOWED ON BEACH
941-861-5000	Siesta Key Beach
	NO DOGS ALLOWED ON BEACH
	South Lido Beach
	NO DOGS ALLOWED ON BEACH
941-964-0375	Stump Pass Beach
	NO DOGS ALLOWED ON BEACH
941-861-5000	Turtle Beach
	NO DOGS ALLOWED ON BEACH
941-488-2236	Venice Municipal Beach
	NO DOGS ALLOWED ON BEACH

Tampa Bay/St. Petersburg Area

727-469-5942	Anclote Key State Park
	NO DOGS ALLOWED ON BEACH
813-931-2121	Ben Davis Municipal Beach
	NO DOGS ALLOWED ON BEACH
727-469-5918	Caladesi Island State Park
	NO DOGS ALLOWED ON BEACH
727-464-3347	Clearwater Beach Island
	NO DOGS ALLOWED ON BEACH
727-462-6963	Clearwater Beach Park
	NO DOGS ALLOWED ON BEACH
813-931-2121	Davis Island
	DOGS ALLOWED ON SOUTH END OF BEACH
813-671-7655	E.G. Simmons Park
	NO DOGS ALLOWED ON SWIMMING BEACH
727-582-2267	Fort DeSoto County Park
	NO DOGS ALLOWED ON BEACH BUT PAST PARK LIMIT THERE IS BEACH ACCESS ON PINELLAS BAYWAY; ALSO DOG BEACH
727-943-4081	Fred Howard Par
	NO DOGS ALLOWED ON BEACH
727-461-6963	Gandy Boulevard Dog Park
	DOGS ALLOWED ON THIS BAY BEACH
727-469-5942	Honeymoon Island State Park
	NO DOGS ALLOWED ON SWIMMING BEACH BUT ARE ALLOWED AT SOUTH BEACH ON LEASH (LEASH MUST REMAIN ON DOG IN WATER BUT NEED NOT BE HELD)
727-588-4852	Indian Rocks Beach
	NO DOGS ALLOWED ON BEACH
727-549-6165	Indian Shores
	NO DOGS ALLOWED ON BEACH
727-391-6111	John Pass Beach
	NO DOGS ALLOWED ON BEACH
727-549-6165	Madeira Beach
	NO DOGS ALLOWED ON BEACH
727-464-3347	Mandalay Park
	NO DOGS ALLOWED ON BEACH
727-367-2735	Pass-a-Grille Beach
	NO DOGS ALLOWED ON BEACH
727-549-6165	Redington Shores County Park
	NO DOGS ALLOWED ON BEACH
727-588-4852	Sand Key Park
	NO DOGS ALLOWED ON BEACH
727-866-2484	St. Petersburg Beach
	NO DOGS ALLOWED ON BEACH
727-549-6165	Treasure Island
	NO DOGS ALLOWED ON BEACH

EMERALD COAST

<u>Gulf Islands National Seashore</u>
850-934-2600   *NO DOGS ALLOWED ON BEACH*

Fort Walton Beach Area
850-837-4540   Destin Beach
                         NO DOGS ALLOWED ON BEACH
850-231-4210   Grayton Beach State Park
                         NO DOGS ALLOWED ON BEACH
850-837-7550   Henderson Beach State Park
                         NO DOGS ALLOWED ON BEACH
850-651-7515   John C. Beasley Park
                         NO DOGS ALLOWED ON BEACH
                         Okaloosa Island Pier
                         NO DOGS ALLOWED ON BEACH
                         Ross Marler Park
                         NO DOGS ALLOWED ON BEACH
850-267-0683   Silver Beach
                         NO DOGS ALLOWED ON BEACH

Panama City Area   Carrabelle Beach
850-697-2585   **DOGS ALLOWED ON BEACH**
850-653-9419   Dr. Julian G. Bruce Beach
                         DOGS ALLOWED ON BEACH
850-235-1159   Mexico Beach
                         NO DOGS ALLOWED ON BEACH
850-233-5045   Panama City Beach
                         NO DOGS ALLOWED ON BEACH
850-233-5140   Saint Andrews State Park
                         NO DOGS ALLOWED ON GULF BEACH
                         BUT CAN GO ON GRAND LAGOON BEACH
850-927-2111   St. George Island State Park
                         LEASHED DOGS ALLOWED ON BEACH
850-227-1327   St. Joseph Peninsula State Park
                         NO DOGS ALLOWED ON BEACH
850-953-9893   St. Vincent National Wildlife Refuge
                         NO DOGS ALLOWED ON ISLAND

Pensacola Area   Big Lagoon State Park
850-492-1595   *NO DOGS ALLOWED ON BEACH*
850-983-1866   Casino Beach/East Park/Johnson Beach
                         NO DOGS ALLOWED ON BEACH
850-492-1595   Fort Pickens/Langdon Beach/Opal Beach
                         NO DOGS ALLOWED ON BEACH
850-983-1866   Navarre Beach
                         NO DOGS ALLOWED ON BEACH
850-983-1866   Pensacola Beach
                         NO DOGS ALLOWED ON BEACH
850-492-1595   Perdido Key State Park
                         NO DOGS ALLOWED ON BEACH BUT CAN
                         GO ON TRAILS

Alabama

For dog owners, Alabama may as well not even have the few beaches it does on the Gulf of Mexico.

Daphne 251-621-3703	Municipal Pier *NO DOGS ALLOWED ON BEACH*
Dauphin Island 251-861-6992	Public Beach *NO DOGS ALLOWED ON BEACH*
Fairhope 251-928-2136	Municipal Beach **DOGS ALLOWED ON BEACH**
Gulf Shores 251-948-7275 251-974-1510	Gulf State Park *NO DOGS ALLOWED ON BEACH* Town Beach *NO DOGS ALLOWED ON BEACH*
Orange Beach 251-981-6979	Town Beach *NO DOGS ALLOWED ON BEACH*

"Dog. A kind of additional or subsidiary
Deity designed to catch the overflow and surplus of the
world's worship."
-Ambrose Bierce

Mississippi

For dog owners, stay on the western coast in Hancock County; dogs aren't allowed around the populated Biloxi beaches.

<u>Gulf Islands National Seashore</u>
228-875-9057   *NO DOGS ALLOWED ON BEACH*

Bay St. Louis   Town Beach
228-467-9092   **LEASHED DOGS ALLOWED ON BEACH**

Biloxi   Town Beach
228-896-6699   *NO DOGS ALLOWED ON BEACH*

Ocean Springs   Davis Bayou Beach
228-875-4424   **DOGS ALLOWED ON BEACH**

Waveland   Waveland Public Beach
228-463-9222   **LEASHED DOGS ALLOWED ON BEACH**

"He is very imprudent, a dog is. He never makes it his business to inquire whether you are in the right or in the wrong, never bothers as to whether you are going up or down upon life's ladder, never asks whether you are rich or poor, silly or wise, sinner or saint.""
-Jerome K. Jerome

Louisiana

People don't seek out Louisiana for its sandy beaches; most of the coastline is made up of bayous. Grand Isle State Park is the only state park with access to the Gulf of Mexico.

Port Fourchon
985-632-6701

Fourchon Beach
THERE ARE NO RESTRICTIONS ON DOGS ON THIS BEACH

Grand Isle
985-787-2559

Grand Isle State Park
LEASHED DOGS ALLOWED IN NON-SWIMMING AREAS

"To err is human, to forgive, canine."
-Anonymous

Texas

If you have been driving along the Gulf Coast, heading west, it has been a long trip for your water-loving dog. But the wait is over in Teaxas...

Recommended Tail-Friendly Beaches

- **Bolivar Peninsula.** Many miles of open beach near Galveston Island; check in at the towns of Bolivar and Crystal Beach if you require civilization.

- **Galveston.** The sand in front of the breakwater is not the prettiest but your dog certainly won't mind. Since the surf is gentle most of the time it is hard to imagine this was the site of America's worst natural disaster when more than 6,000 people died in the aftermath of a storm on September 8-9, 1900. The oldest part of the 10-mile seawall built to protect the city is still visible from 6th Street to 39th Street and dates to 1902.

- **Padre Island.** Padre Island is America's longest barrier island - there is plenty of room for dogs to roam on its 113 miles of sand. One of the best places for a dog anywhere.

Padre Island National Seashore
361-949-8173   **DOGS ARE ALLOWED ANYWHERE EXCEPT ON THE DECK AT MALAQUITE BEACH AND IN FRONT OF THE VISITOR CENTER AT THE SWIMMING BEACH**

Bolivar
409-684-5940   Town Beach
DOGS ALLOWED ON ISLAND BEACHES

Crystal Beach
409-684-5940   Town Beach
DOGS ALLOWED ON ISLAND BEACHES

Galveston
409-762-3278   East Beach
409-737-1222   **LEASHED DOGS ALLOWED ON BEACH**
Galveston Island State Park
LEASHED DOGS ALLOWED ON BEACH
888-425-4753   Stewart Beach Park
LEASHED DOGS ALLOWED ON BEACH

Port Arsanas 361-749-4111	Mustang Island State Park **LEASHED DOGS ALLOWED ON BEACH**
Port O'Connor 361-983-2215	Matagorda Island State Park **LEASHED DOGS ALLOWED ON BEACH**
Sabine Pass 409-971-2559	Sea Rim State Park **LEASHED DOGS ALLOWED ON BEACH**
South Padre Island 800-SOPADRE	Town Beach **LEASHED DOGS ALLOWED ON BEACH; UNLEASHED NORTH OF TOWN**

"Happiness is dog-shaped."
-Chapman Pincher

Your Dog On The
Pacific Ocean
Beaches...

California

Northern California is more friendly than Southern California. As the waters warm up heading south, the beaches become more restrictive. By the time you reach Los Angeles, don't expect to find any place to get your dog onto the sand. Beaches in the state can close to dogs with little warning due to nesting sites set up by the snowy plover, a small shorebird that is listed as a threatened species.

Recommended Tail-Friendly Beaches

- **Crescent Beach.** Dogs aren't allowed to poke around Redwoods National Park too much but they are allowed on this wide semi-circle of sand. The waves in the broad cove usually lap softly onto the shore but this was the site of a tsunami that wrecked Crescent City in 1964. A century earlier, the sidewheeler *Brother Jonathan* struck a submerged rock spire known as the "Dragon's Teeth." Lifeboats were deployed but only one made it to shore with 19 survivors. The loss of 215 lives remains the worst maritime disaster in California history.

- **Mendocino.** The bluffs around the Northern California town are the main attraction but your dog will favor the state park beaches in the area instead.

- **Point Reyes.** You just can't hit the beach with your dog at the national seashore - there are restrictions for that snowy plover at certain times and elephant seal mating at other times and other beach restrictions but there is also plenty of open sand and interesting terrain around the peninsula for your dog.

- **Golden Gate National Recreation Area.** In 1972 a menagerie of government properties around the San Francisco Bay that included forts, a prison, an airfield, beaches and forests were knitted into one of the world's largest urban national parks. Much of it is open to your dog. Start on Fort Funston on the Pacific Ocean and work your way around the bay. The north end of Stinson Beach in Marin County is a dog beach.

Carmel-by-the-Sea. You will never find a more dog-friendly beach than Carmel Beach where dogs and people mingle freely on soft white sand. This is the biggest beach among the craggy headlands of Monterey Peninsula. Dogs are also welcome on Carmel River State Beach at the east end of town.

Pfeiffer Beach. The Big Sur coastline south of the Monterey Peninsula is a must-see for any traveler. A string of state parks provides the best access to seascapes that Rovert Louis Stevenson described famously as "the greatest meeting of land and sea in the world." Your dog, sadly, will not be able to confirm that since the Big Sur state parks ban dogs for the most part. But Big Sur is not a complete washout for dog lovers, however. A short, sandy trail leads to Pfeiffer Beach, one of the most beautiful public beaches in California. The sand is wrapped in spectacular rock formations making this a very secluded beach indeed. The rocks are sprinkled in the surf as well, forming coves and making for exciting play in the waves for dogs. The turn-off from Highway 1 is obscured and easy to miss on the crest of a hill so be diligent when seeking out Pfeiffer Beach.

Pismo Beach. A good, hassle-free beach to bring your dog on the Central Coast. When you see trucks lining up to drive on the beach, you can assume no one is going to much mind about your dog. Convenient parking in town as well.

San Simeon. William Randolph Hearst's beach at the foot of his castle is not dramatic or expansive by California standards but your dog won't be critical. Just pull off Highway 1, walk down some wooden steps and you are on the beach in about one minute. The beach in front of the short, grassy bluffs is a mix of stones and rocks and a strip of sand.

San Diego's Dog Beach (North Beach). With 38 acres at the north end of Ocean Beach, Dog Beach is the second largest leash-free beach for dogs in America. City officials estimate that as many as 10,000 dogs visit each week.

Cardiff
760-753-5091

Cardiff State Beach
LEASHED DOGS ALLOWED ON BEACH FROM SOUTH END OF SAN ELIJO LAGOON TO SOLANA BEACH
San Elijo State Beach
LEASHED DOGS ALLOWED ON BEACH FROM SWAMI'S BEACH TO SAN ELIJO LAGOON MOUTH

Carlsbad
760-438-3143
760-438-2675

Carlsbad State Beach
NO DOGS ALLOWED ON BEACH
South Carlsbad State Beach
NO DOGS ALLOWED ON BEACH

Coronado

Coronado Beach
DOGS ALLOWED ON BEACH ONLY IN A NARROW CORRIDOR FROM OCEAN BOULEVARD ALONG FENCE AT NORTH ISLAND NAVAL AIR STATION GATE 5

Del Mar
858-755-1556

Del Mar City Beach
NO DOGS ALLOWED ON BEACH
North Beach
FROM VIA DE LA VALLE TO 27TH STREET DOGS ALLOWED ON BEACH UNDER VOICE CONTROL FROM SEPT 15 TO JUN 15; ALLOWED LEASHED ON BEACH OTHERWISE

Encinitas
760-633-2750

Beacons Beach
NO DOGS ALLOWED ON BEACH
Boneyard Beach
NO DOGS ALLOWED ON BEACH
D Street Beach
NO DOGS ALLOWED ON BEACH
Encinitas Beach
NO DOGS ALLOWED ON BEACH
Moonlight Beach
NO DOGS ALLOWED ON BEACH
Stone Steps Beach
NO DOGS ALLOWED ON BEACH
Swami's
NO DOGS ALLOWED ON BEACH

Imperial Beach 619-423-8328	Imperial Beach **LEASHED DOGS ALLOWED SOUTH OF IMPERIAL BEACH BOULEVARD AND NOT ALLOWED NORTH OF IMPERIAL BEACH BOULEVARD**
619-435-5184	Silver Strand State Beach *NO DOGS ALLOWED ON BEACH*
La Jolla 619-221-8899	Black's Beach *NO DOGS ALLOWED ON BEACH* Marine Street Beach **LEASHED DOGS ALLOWED ON BEACH BEFORE 9 AM AND AFTER 6 PM** Windansea Beach **LEASHED DOGS ALLOWED ON BEACH BEFORE 9 AM AND AFTER 6 PM**
Mission Beach 619-221-8899	Mission Beach **LEASHED DOGS ALLOWED ON BEACH BEFORE 9 AM AND AFTER 6 PM**
Oceanside 760-435-4018	Buccaneer Beach *NO DOGS ALLOWED ON BEACH* Oceanside City Beach *NO DOGS ALLOWED ON BEACH*
Pacific Beach 619-221-8899	Pacific Beach **LEASHED DOGS ALLOWED ON BEACH BEFORE 9 AM AND AFTER 6 PM** Tourmaline Surfing Park **LEASHED DOGS ALLOWED ON BEACH BEFORE 9 AM AND AFTER 6 PM**
San Diego 619-221-8899	Ocean Beach **LEASHED DOGS ALLOWED ON BEACH BEFORE 9 AM AND AFTER 6 PM; DOGS ALLOWED OFF-LEASH NORTH OF THE BICYCLE PATH THAT TERMINATES ON THE NORTH EDGE OF THE VOLTAIRE STREET PARKING LOT**
Solana Beach 858-755-1569	Delmar Shores Beach Park *NO DOGS ALLOWED ON BEACH* Fletcher Cove Beach Park *NO DOGS ALLOWED ON BEACH* Seascape Surf Beach Park *NO DOGS ALLOWED ON BEACH* Tide Beach Park *NO DOGS ALLOWED ON BEACH*

Balboa
949-644-3309

Balboa Beach
NO DOGS ALLOWED ON BEACH
Balboa Island
NO DOGS ALLOWED ON BEACH
West Jetty View Park
NO DOGS ALLOWED ON BEACH

Capistrano Beach
949-661-7013

Capistrano Beach
NO DOGS ALLOWED ON BEACH
Poche Beach
NO DOGS ALLOWED ON BEACH

Corona del Mar
949-722-1611

949-644-3044

Corona del Mar State Beach
**LEASHED DOGS ALLOWED ON BEACH
BEFORE 9 AM AND AFTER 9 PM**
Little Corona del Mar Beach
LEASHED DOGS ALLOWED ON BEACH

Dana Point
949-496-1094
949-496-6171

Dana Point Harbor Beach
NO DOGS ALLOWED ON BEACH
Doheny State Beach
NO DOGS ALLOWED ON BEACH

Huntington Beach
714-846-3460
714-536-5486

714-536-1454

Bolsa Chica State Beach
NO DOGS ALLOWED ON BEACH
Huntington City Beach
**DOGS ALLOWED ON "DOG BEACH" AT
THE NORTHERNMOST POINT AT
SEAPOINT AVENUE**
Huntington State Beach
NO DOGS ALLOWED ON BEACH

Laguna Beach
714-494-6572

714-494-3539

714-497-0706

714-494-6572

Brooks Beach
**FROM JUNE 1-SEPT 15 LEASHED DOGS
ALLOWED ON BEACH ONLY BEFORE
8 AM AND AFTER 6 PM; LEASHED DOGS
ALLOWED ANYTIME OTHERWISE**
Crystal Cove State Park
NO DOGS ALLOWED ON BEACH
Main Beach
**FROM JUNE 1-SEPT 15 LEASHED DOGS
ALLOWED ON BEACH ONLY BEFORE
8 AM AND AFTER 6 PM; LEASHED DOGS
ALLOWED ANYTIME OTHERWISE**
Victoria Beach
**FROM JUNE 1-SEPT 15 LEASHED DOGS
ALLOWED ON BEACH ONLY BEFORE
8 AM AND AFTER 6 PM; LEASHED DOGS
ALLOWED ANYTIME OTHERWISE**

Newport Beach	Los Alenas Park
949-644-3044	*NO DOGS ALLOWED ON BEACH*
949-644-3309	Newport Beach/West Newport Beach
	NO DOGS ALLOWED ON BEACH
949-723-4511	Santa Ana River County Beach
	NO DOGS ALLOWED ON BEACH
San Clemente	Calafia Beach
949-361-8264	*NO DOGS ALLOWED ON BEACH*
	North Beach
	NO DOGS ALLOWED ON BEACH
	San Clemente City Beach
	NO DOGS ALLOWED ON BEACH
949-492-0802	San Clemente State Beach
	NO DOGS ALLOWED ON BEACH
949-492-4872	San Onofre State Beach
	NO DOGS ALLOWED ON BEACH
Seal Beach	Seal Beach
310-430-2527	*NO DOGS ALLOWED ON BEACH*
South Laguna	Aliso Beach County Park
949-497-0706	**FROM JUNE 1 THROUGH SEPT 15 LEASHED DOGS ALLOWED ON BEACH ONLY BEFORE 8 AM AND AFTER 6 PM; LEASHED DOGS ALLOWED ON BEACH ANYTIME THE REST OF THE YEAR**
949-661-7013	Camel Point Beach
	FROM JUNE 1 THROUGH SEPT 15 LEASHED DOGS ALLOWED ON BEACH ONLY BEFORE 8 AM AND AFTER 6 PM; LEASHED DOGS ALLOWED ON BEACH ANYTIME THE REST OF THE YEAR
	Salt Creek Beach Park
	NO DOGS ALLOWED ON BEACH
	1,000 Steps Beach
	FROM JUNE 1 THROUGH SEPT 15 LEASHED DOGS ALLOWED ON BEACH ONLY BEFORE 8 AM AND AFTER 6 PM; LEASHED DOGS ALLOWED ON BEACH ANYTIME THE REST OF THE YEAR
Sunset Beach	Sunset Beach
949-509-6683	*NO DOGS ALLOWED ON BEACH*
Surfside	Surfside Beach
310-430-2613	*NO DOGS ALLOWED ON BEACH*

SOUTHERN COAST - LOS ANGELES COUNTY

Catalina Island
310-305-9546
310-510-1520

Avalon Bay Beach
DOGS CAN GO ON ISLAND BUT NOT BEACH
Ben Watson Beach
DOGS CAN GO ON ISLAND BUT NOT BEACH
Crescent Beach
DOGS CAN GO ON ISLAND BUT NOT BEACH
Descanso Beach
DOGS CAN GO ON ISLAND BUT NOT BEACH
Little Harbor Beach
DOGS CAN GO ON ISLAND BUT NOT BEACH
Pebbly Beach
DOGS CAN GO ON ISLAND BUT NOT BEACH

Hermosa Beach
310-372-2166

Hermosa Beach
NO DOGS ALLOWED ON BEACH

Long Beach
562-570-3100

Alamitos Bay Beach
NO DOGS ALLOWED ON BEACH
Belmont Shore Beach
DOGS ALLOWED OFF-LEASH IN 3-ACRE AREA BETWEEN ROYCROFT AND ARGONNE AVENUES BETWEEN 6 AM AND 8 PM

562-570-3215

White Point County Park
NO DOGS ALLOWED ON BEACH

Malibu
310-457-9891
310-457-2525

Amarillo Beach
NO DOGS ALLOWED ON BEACH
Dan Blocker County Beach
NO DOGS ALLOWED ON BEACH

818-880-0350

El Matador State Beach
NO DOGS ALLOWED ON BEACH
El Pescador State Beach
NO DOGS ALLOWED ON BEACH
La Piedra State Beach
NO DOGS ALLOWED ON BEACH

310-394-3261

Las Tunas County Beach
NO DOGS ALLOWED ON BEACH

818-880-0530

Leo Carillo State Beach
LEASHED DOGS ALLOWED ON BEACH EXCEPT BETWEEN LIFEGUARD STAND 1 AN 3 BECAUSE OF TIDEPOOLS

Malibu	Malibu Lagoon County Beach
310-305-9546	*NO DOGS ALLOWED ON BEACH*
	Nicholas Canyon County Beach
	NO DOGS ALLOWED ON BEACH
310-457-2511	Paradise Cove
	NO DOGS ALLOWED ON BEACH
310-457-2525	Point Dume County Beach
	NO DOGS ALLOWED ON BEACH
	Surfrider Beach
310-457-2525	*NO DOGS ALLOWED ON BEACH*
310-372-2166	Topanga County Beach
	NO DOGS ALLOWED ON BEACH
	Zuma County Beach
	NO DOGS ALLOWED ON BEACH
Manhattan Beach	Manhattan County Beach
310-372-2166	*NO DOGS ALLOWED ON BEACH*
Marina del Rey	Marina Beach
310-344-3261	*NO DOGS ALLOWED ON BEACH*
Palos Verdes Estates	Abalone Cove Beach
310-377-0360	*NO DOGS ALLOWED ON BEACH*
310-372-2166	Malaga Cove Beach
	NO DOGS ALLOWED ON BEACH
	Royal Palms County Beach
	NO DOGS ALLOWED ON BEACH
Playa del Rey	Dockweiler State Beach
310-372-2166	*NO DOGS ALLOWED ON BEACH*
	Playa del Rey Beach
	NO DOGS ALLOWED ON BEACH
Redondo Beach	Redondo County Beach
310-372-2166	*NO DOGS ALLOWED ON BEACH*
	Torrance County Beach
	NO DOGS ALLOWED ON BEACH
San Pedro	Cabrillo City Beach
310-548-2914	*NO DOGS ALLOWED ON BEACH*
310-372-2166	White Point County Park
	NO DOGS ALLOWED ON BEACH
Santa Monica	Santa Monica State Beach
310-578-0478	*NO DOGS ALLOWED ON BEACH*
310-372-2166	Will Rogers State Beach
	NO DOGS ALLOWED ON BEACH
Venice	Venice City Beach
310-372-2166	*NO DOGS ALLOWED ON BEACH*

CENTRAL COAST - VENTURA COUNTY

Oxnard
805-382-3007

Hollywood Beach
**LEASHED DOGS ALLOWED ON
BEACH BETWEEN 5 PM AND 9 AM**

805-654-3951

Mandalay County Park
LEASHED DOGS ALLOWED ON BEACH

805-654-4744

McGrath State Beach
NO DOGS ALLOWED ON BEACH

805-385-7950

Oxnard Beach Park
LEASHED DOGS ALLOWED ON BEACH

805-382-3007

Silver Strand Beach
**LEASHED DOGS ALLOWED ON BEACH
BETWEEN 5 PM AND 9 AM**

Port Hueneme
818-880-0350

Point Magu State Park
LEASHED DOGS ALLOWED ON BEACH

Ventura
805-658-5700
805-968-1033

Channel Islands National Park
NO DOGS ALLOWED ON ISLANDS
Emma Wood State Beach
LEASHED DOGS ALLOWED ON BEACH

805-654-3951

Faria Beach County Park
LEASHED DOGS ALLOWED ON BEACH
Hobson County Park
LEASHED DOGS ALLOWED ON BEACH

805-652-4550

Marina Park
LEASHED DOGS ALLOWED ON BEACH

805-899-1400

San Buenaventura State Beach
NO DOGS ALLOWED ON BEACH

805-654-7800

Surfer's Point at Seaside
LEASHED DOGS ALLOWED ON BEACH

CENTRAL COAST - SANTA BARBARA COUNTY

Carpinteria
805-684-5405
805-684-2811

Carpinteria City Beach
NO DOGS ALLOWED ON BEACH
Carpinteria State Beach
NO DOGS ALLOWED ON BEACH

805-684-5405

Jellybowl Beach
LEASHED DOGS ALLOWED ON BEACH
Rincon Beach County Park

805-681-5650
805-684-5405

LEASHED DOGS ALLOWED ON BEACH
Rincon Point Beach
NO DOGS ALLOWED ON BEACH
Santa Claus Lane Beach
NO DOGS ALLOWED ON BEACH

Goleta
805-968-1033

El Capitan State Beach
NO DOGS ALLOWED ON BEACH
Gaviota State Park
NO DOGS ALLOWED ON BEACH

Goleta	Goleta Beach County Park
805-967-1300	**LEASHED DOGS ALLOWED ON BEACH**
	Isla Vista Beach
	NO DOGS ALLOWED ON BEACH
805-968-1033	Refugio State Beach
	NO DOGS ALLOWED ON BEACH

| Guadalupe | Rancho Guadalupe Dunes County Park |
| 805-934-6123 | **LEASHED DOGS ALLOWED ON BEACH** |

Lompoc	Jalama Beach County Park
805-736-6316	**LEASHED DOGS ALLOWED ON BEACH**
805-934-6123	Ocean Beach County Park
	LEASHED DOGS ALLOWED ON BEACH

Santa Barbara	Arroyo Burro Beach County Park
805-687-3714	**LEASHED DOGS ALLOWED ON BEACH**
805-564-5418	Butterfly Beach
	NO DOGS ALLOWED ON BEACH
	East Beach
	NO DOGS ALLOWED ON BEACH
	Leadbetter Beach
	NO DOGS ALLOWED ON BEACH
	Mesa Lane Beach
	NO DOGS ALLOWED ON BEACH
	Thousand Steps Beach
	NO DOGS ALLOWED ON BEACH
	West Beach
	NO DOGS ALLOWED ON BEACH

Summerland	Lookout County Beach
805-969-1720	*NO DOGS ALLOWED ON BEACH*
805-568-2461	Summerland Beach
	DOGS ALLOWED ON BEACH

CENTRAL COAST - SAN LUIS OBISPO COUNTY

| Cambria | Moonstone State Beach |
| 805-927-3624 | **LEASHED DOGS ALLOWED ON BEACH** |

Cayucos	Cayucos State Beach
805-781-5200	**LEASHED DOGS ALLOWED ON BEACH**
805-772-2560	Morrow Strand State Beach
	LEASHED DOGS ALLOWED ON BEACH IN DESIGNATED AREAS

Pismo Beach	Avila Beach
805-773-2208	**LEASHED DOGS ALLOWED ON BEACH BEFORE 10 AM AND 5 PM**
	Oceano Beach
	LEASHED DOGS ALLOWED ON BEACH

Pismo Beach	Olde Port Beach
805-773-2208	**LEASHED DOGS ALLOWED ON BEACH**
	Pismo State Beach
805-489-2684	**LEASHED DOGS ALLOWED ON BEACH**
805-773-4382	Shell Beach
	LEASHED DOGS ALLOWED ON BEACH
San Simeon	San Simeon State Beach
805-927-2020	**LEASHED DOGS ALLOWED ON BEACH**
	W.R. Hearst Memorial State Beach
	LEASHED DOGS ALLOWED ON BEACH

CENTRAL COAST - MONTEREY COUNTY

Big Sur	Andrew Molera State Park
831-667-2315	*NO DOGS ALLOWED ON BEACH*
	Garrapata State Park
	NO DOGS ALLOWED ON BEACH
	Julia Pfeiffer Burns State Park
	NO DOGS ALLOWED ON BEACH
831-667-2403	Limekiln State Park
	NO DOGS ALLOWED ON BEACH
831-667-2315	Pfeiffer Beach
	LEASHED DOGS ALLOWED ON BEACH
Carmel	Carmel City Beach
831-624-3543	**DOGS ALLOWED OFF-LEASH ON BEACH**
831-649-2836	Carmel River State Beach
	LEASHED DOGS ALLOWED ON BEACH
	Point Lobos State Reserve
	LEASHED DOGS ALLOWED ON BEACH
Marina	Marina State Beach
831-384-7695	**LEASHED DOGS ALLOWED ON BEACH**
Moss Landing	Moss Landing State Beach
831-649-2836	**LEASHED DOGS ALLOWED ON BEACH**
	Salinas River State Beach
	LEASHED DOGS ALLOWED ON BEACH
	Zmudowski State Beach
	LEASHED DOGS ALLOWED ON BEACH
Monterey	Macabee Beach
831-646-3866	**LEASHED DOGS ALLOWED ON BEACH**
831-646-8860	Monterey StateBeach
	LEASHED DOGS ALLOWED ON BEACH
831-646-3866	San Carlos Beach Park
	LEASHED DOGS ALLOWED ON BEACH

Pacific Grove 831-372-4076 831-648-3130	Asilomar State Beach **LEASHED DOGS ALLOWED ON BEACH** Lover's Point **LEASHED DOGS ALLOWED ON BEACH** Shoreline Park **LEASHED DOGS ALLOWED ON BEACH**
Pebble Beach 831-646-3866	Fanshell Beach **LEASHED DOGS ALLOWED ON BEACH** Moss Beach **LEASHED DOGS ALLOWED ON BEACH** Spanish Bay **LEASHED DOGS ALLOWED ON BEACH**
Seaside 831-394-3054	Sand Public Beach **LEASHED DOGS ALLOWED ON BEACH**

CENTRAL COAST - SANTA CRUZ COUNTY

Aptos 831-688-1467 831-761-1795 831-429-2850 831-685-6500	Lundborgh Beach **LEASHED DOGS ALLOWED ON BEACH** Manresa State Beach **LEASHED DOGS ALLOWED ON BEACH** Manresa Uplands **LEASHED DOGS ALLOWED ON BEACH** Rio Del Mar Beach **LEASHED DOGS ALLOWED ON BEACH** Seacliff State Beach **LEASHED DOGS ALLOWED ON BEACH; FURTHER SOUTH AT SEASCAPE DOGS CAN USUALLY RUN FREE**
Capitola 831-475-7300 831-464-6330	Capitola City Beach *NO DOGS ALLOWED ON BEACH* New Brighton State Beach *LEASHED DOGS ALLOWED ON TRAILS ABOVE BEACH BUT NOT ON BEACH*
Davenport 650-879-2025 831-462-8333	Ano Nuevo State Reserve *NO DOGS ALLOWED ON BEACH* Bonny Doon Beach **LEASHED DOGS ALLOWED ON BEACH** Davenport Beach **LEASHED DOGS ALLOWED ON BEACH** Davenport Landing Beach **LEASHED DOGS ALLOWED ON BEACH** Panther Beach **LEASHED DOGS ALLOWED ON BEACH** Scott Creek Beach **LEASHED DOGS ALLOWED ON BEACH** Yellowbank Beach **LEASHED DOGS ALLOWED ON BEACH**

Santa Cruz 831-420-6015	Corcoran Lagoon Beach *NO DOGS ALLOWED ON BEACH* Cowell Beach *NO DOGS ALLOWED ON BEACH OR* *BOARDWALK* Hooper Beach *NO DOGS ALLOWED ON BEACH* Key Beach *NO DOGS ALLOWED ON BEACH*
831-420-5670	Lighthouse Field State Beach **DOGS ALLOWED ON BEACH OFF-LEASH** **SUNRISE TO 10 AM AND 4 PM TO** **SUNSET**
831-420-6015	Lincoln Beach *NO DOGS ALLOWED ON BEACH* Main Beach
831-420-6015	*NO DOGS ALLOWED ON BEACH OR* *BOARDWALK* Mitchell's Cove **DOGS ALLOWED OFF-LEASH ON BEACH**
831-462-8333	Moran Lake Beach **LEASHED DOGS ALLOWED ON BEACH**
831-423-4609	Natural Bridges State Beach **LEASHED DOGS ALLOWED ON BEACH**
831-462-8333	Pleasure Point Beach *NO DOGS ALLOWED ON BEACH*
831-429-2850	Seabright Beach **DOGS ALLOWED ON BEACH**
831-420-6015	Steamer Lane *NO DOGS ALLOWED ON BEACH* Sunny Cove *NO DOGS ALLOWED ON BEACH*
831-429-2850	Twin Lakes State Beach **DOGS ALLOWED ON BEACH**
Watsonville 831-763-7062	Sunset State Beach **LEASHED DOGS ALLOWED ON BEACH IN** **DESIGNATED AREAS**

Daly City 650-991-5101	Esplanade Beach **DOGS ALLOWED OFF-LEASH ON BEACH**
Half Moon Bay 650-726-8819	Cowell Ranch Beach **LEASHED DOGS ALLOWED ON BEACH** Dunes Beach **LEASHED DOGS ALLOWED ON BEACH** El Granada Beach **LEASHED DOGS ALLOWED ON BEACH** Francis Beach *NO DOGS ALLOWED ON BEACH*
650-726-4357	Martin's Beach **LEASHED DOGS ALLOWED ON BEACH**
650-726-8819	Mirimar Beach **LEASHED DOGS ALLOWED ON BEACH** Pelican Point Beach **LEASHED DOGS ALLOWED ON BEACH** Venice Beach **LEASHED DOGS ALLOWED ON BEACH**
Montara 650-728-5336 650-726-8819	Gray Whale Cove State Beach **LEASHED DOGS ALLOWED ON BEACH** Montara State Beach **LEASHED DOGS ALLOWED ON BEACH**
Moss Beach 650-728-3584	James V. Fitzgerald Marine Reserve *NO DOGS ALLOWED ON BEACH*
Pacifica 650-738-7381 650-738-7380	Pacifica State Beach **LEASHED DOGS ALLOWED ON BEACH** Rockaway Beach **LEASHED DOGS ALLOWED ON BEACH** Sharp Park Beach **DOGS ALLOWED OFF-LEASH ON BEACH**
Pescadero 650-879-2170	Bean Hollow State Beach **LEASHED DOGS ALLOWED ON BEACH** Gazos Creek Access **LEASHED DOGS ALLOWED ON BEACH** Pebble Beach **LEASHED DOGS ALLOWED ON BEACH** Pescadero State Beach **LEASHED DOGS ALLOWED ON BEACH** Pigeon Point Beach **LEASHED DOGS ALLOWED ON BEACH**
San Gregorio 650-879-2170	Pomponio State Beach **LEASHED DOGS ALLOWED ON BEACH** San Gregorio State Beach **LEASHED DOGS ALLOWED ON BEACH**

NORTH COAST - SAN FRANCISCO COUNTY

Golden Gate National Recreation Area
415-561-4700   China Beach
                      NO DOGS ALLOWED ON BEACH
                      Crissy Field
                      **LEASHED DOGS PERMITTED EXCEPT IN
                      WILDLIFE PROTECTION AREAS; DOGS
                      NOT PERMITTED ON LOTOS CREEK
                      BOARDWALK**
                      Fort Funston
                      **LEASHED DOGS ALLOWED EXCEPT IN
                      WILDLIFE PROTECTION AREAS**
                      Lands End Beach
                      LEASHED DOGS ALLOWED ON BEACH
                      Muir Beach
                      **LEASHED DOGS ALLOWED IN
                      DESIGNATED AREAS; NOT ALLOWED
                      IN LAGOON OR REDWOOD CREEK**
                      Ocean Beach
                      **LEASHED DOGS ALLOWED EXCEPT IN
                      WILDLIFE PROTECTION AREAS**

San Francisco   Baker Beach
650-556-8371   **DOGS ALLOWED OFF LEASH ON BEACH**

NORTH COAST - MARIN COUNTY

Bolinas   Agate Beach
650-499-6387   **DOGS ALLOWED ON BEACH UNDER
                      VOICE CONTROL**
                      Bolinas Beach
                      LEASHED DOGS ALLOWED ON BEACH
                      RCA Beach
                      LEASHED DOGS ALLOWED ON BEACH

Sausalito   Dunphy Park
415-289-4125   **LEASHED DOGS ALLOWED ON BAY
                      BEACH**
415-331-1540   Marin Headlands
                      LEASHED DOGS ALLOWED ON BEACH
                      Rodeo Beach
                      **DOGS ALLOWED OFF LEASH FROM
                      SHORELINE TO THE CREST OF THE
                      DUNES**

Stinson Beach   Dog Beach/Stinson Beach
415-868-0942   **DOGS ALLOWED ON BEACH AT NORTH
                      END OF STINSON BEACH**
415-388-2070   Red Rock Beach
                      NO DOGS ALLOWED ON BEACH

NORTH COAST - SONOMA COUNTY

Bodega Bay 707-875-3483 707-875-3866	Arched Rock Beach **LEASHED DOGS ALLOWED ON BEACH** Bodega Dunes Beach *NO DOGS ALLOWED ON BEACH* Bodega Head *NO DOGS ALLOWED ON BEACH* Coleman Beach **LEASHED DOGS ALLOWED ON BEACH**
707-875-3540	Doran Beach Regional Park **LEASHED DOGS ALLOWED ON BEACH**
707-875-3866	Miwok Beach *NO DOGS ALLOWED ON BEACH* North Salmon Creek Beach
707-875-3866	**DOGS ALLOWED ON BEACH** South Salmon Creek Beach *NO DOGS ALLOWED ON BEACH*
Carmet 707-875-3483	Carmet Beach **LEASHED DOGS ALLOWED ON BEACH** Portugese Beach **LEASHED DOGS ALLOWED ON BEACH** Schoolhouse Beach **LEASHED DOGS ALLOWED ON BEACH**
Jenner 707-875-3483	Blind Beach **LEASHED DOGS ALLOWED ON BEACH** Goat Rock Beach *NO DOGS ALLOWED ON BEACH*
707-847-3221	Salt Point State Beach *NO DOGS ALLOWED ON BEACH*
707-847-3245	Stillwater Cove Regional Park **LEASHED DOGS ALLOWED ON BEACH**
Ocean View 707-875-3483	Gleason Beach **LEASHED DOGS ALLOWED ON BEACH** Shell Beach **LEASHED DOGS ALLOWED ON BEACH** Wright's Beach **LEASHED DOGS ALLOWED ON BEACH**
Sea Ranch 707-785-2377	Black Point Beach **LEASHED DOGS ALLOWED ON BEACH** Pebble Beach **LEASHED DOGS ALLOWED ON BEACH** Shell Beach **LEASHED DOGS ALLOWED ON BEACH** Stengel Beach **LEASHED DOGS ALLOWED ON BEACH** Walk-On Beach **LEASHED DOGS ALLOWED ON BEACH**

Caspar
707-937-5804

Caspar State Beach
LEASHED DOGS ALLOWED ON BEACH

Fort Bragg
707-961-6300
707-964-9112

Glass Beach
LEASHED DOGS ALLOWED ON BEACH
MacKerricher State Park
LEASHED DOGS ALLOWED ON BEACH

707-961-6300

Noyo Harbor Beach
LEASHED DOGS ALLOWED ON BEACH
Pudding Creek Beach
LEASHED DOGS ALLOWED ON BEACH
Virgin Creek Beach
LEASHED DOGS ALLOWED ON BEACH

Gualala
707-834-3533
707-785-2377

Gualala River Beach
DOGS ALLOWED ON BEACH
Gualala Point Regional Park
LEASHED DOGS ALLOWED ON BEACH

Manchester
707-882-2463

Manchester State Beach
LEASHED DOGS ALLOWED ON BEACH

Mendocino
707-937-5804

Mendocino Headlands State Park
LEASHED DOGS ALLOWED ON BEACH
Russian Gulch State Park
LEASHED DOGS ALLOWED ON BEACH
Van Damme State Park
LEASHED DOGS ALLOWED ON BEACH

Point Arena
707-884-3831

Bowling Ball Beach
LEASHED DOGS ALLOWED ON BEACH
Fish Rock Beach
LEASHED DOGS ALLOWED ON BEACH

707-937-5804

Greenwood Creek State Beach
LEASHED DOGS ALLOWED ON BEACH

707-884-3831

Schooner Gulch Beach
LEASHED DOGS ALLOWED ON BEACH

Westport
707-462-4705

Bear Harbor Beach
LEASHED DOGS ALLOWED ON BEACH
Jones Beach
LEASHED DOGS ALLOWED ON BEACH
Little Jackass Creek Beach
LEASHED DOGS ALLOWED ON BEACH
Needle Rock Beach
LEASHED DOGS ALLOWED ON BEACH
Seaside Creek Beach
LEASHED DOGS ALLOWED ON BEACH
Westport-Union Landing State Beach
LEASHED DOGS ALLOWED ON BEACH

King Range National Conservation Area
707-825-2300   Black Sands Beach
DOGS ALLOWED OFF-LEASH ON BEACH
Little Black Sands Beach
DOGS ALLOWED OFF-LEASH ON BEACH
Mattole River Beach
DOGS ALLOWED OFF-LEASH ON BEACH

Arcata   Clam Beach County Park
707-445-7652   **DOGS ALLOWED OFF-LEASH ON BEACH**
707-445-7651   Mad River County Park
DOGS ALLOWED OFF-LEASH ON BEACH

Eureka   Samoa Dunes Recreation Area
707-825-2300   **DOGS ALLOWED OFF-LEASH ON BEACH;
MUST BE LEASHED ON TRAILS**

Ferndale   Centerville Beach County Park
800-346-3482   **DOGS ALLOWED ON BEACH; MUST BE
LEASHED MAR 1 TO SEPT 30**
Crab County Park
**DOGS ALLOWED ON BEACH; MUST BE
LEASHED MAR 1 TO SEPT 30**

Orick   Carruthers Cove Beach
707-825-2300   **DOGS ALLOWED ON BEACH**
707-464-1812   Gold Bluffs Beach
NO DOGS ALLOWED ON BEACH

Trinidad   Agate Beach
707-677-1610   **LEASHED DOGS ALLOWED ON BEACH**
Baker Beach
LEASHED DOGS ALLOWED ON BEACH
800-346-3482   Big Lagoon County Park
LEASHED DOGS ALLOWED ON BEACH
707-677-1610   College Cove
LEASHED DOGS ALLOWED ON BEACH
Indian Beach
LEASHED DOGS ALLOWED ON BEACH
Luffenholtz Beach
LEASHED DOGS ALLOWED ON BEACH
Moonstone Beach
LEASHED DOGS ALLOWED ON BEACH
Trinidad State Beach
LEASHED DOGS ALLOWED ON BEACH

Redwood National Park
707-464-1812
    Crescent Beach
    LEASHED DOGS ALLOWED ON BEACH
    Enderts Beach
    LEASHED DOGS ALLOWED ON BEACH TRAIL
    Wilson Creek Beach
    NO DOGS ALLOWED ON BEACH

Crescent City
707-457-3131
    Garth Beach
    LEASHED DOGS ALLOWED ON BEACH, GRASS
    Pebble Beach
    LEASHED DOGS ALLOWED ON BEACH, GRASS
    South Beach
    LEASHED DOGS ALLOWED ON BEACH, GRASS

Smith River
707-464-7230
707-464-6100 x5151
    Clifford Kamph Memorial Park
    LEASHED DOGS ALLOWED ON BEACH
    Pelican State Beach
    LEASHED DOGS ALLOWED ON BEACH

*"What counts is not necessarily the size of the dog
in the fight but the size of the fight in the dog."
-Dwight D. Eisenhower*

Oregon

All of Oregon's beaches are public. You can step on every grain of Oregon sand for 400 miles and, in the rare exception of a ban due to nesting birds, your dog can be with you all the way.

Recommended Tail-Friendly Beaches

Cannon Beach. Withs its views of the sea, the mountains and rugged coastal outcroppings, this is one of Oregon's most celebrated beaches. Haystack Rock looms out in the surf. Come in October for the Dog Show on the Beach.

Gold Beach. The beach where the Rogue River reaches the Pacific ocean is noted for its clean sands. Your dog can help with the beachcombing in the state recreation area.

Oregon Dunes National Recreation Area. These wind-sculpted dunes are the largest expanse of coastal sand dunes in North America. As long as the birds aren't nesting, your dog is allowed anywhere on the sand.

SOUTHERN COAST

Oregon Dunes National Recreation Area
541-271-3611   **LEASHED DOGS ALLOWED ON BEACH**

Bandon   Bandon State Natural Area
800-551-6949   **LEASHED DOGS ALLOWED ON BEACH**
541-347-2209   Bullards Beach State Park
                LEASHED DOGS ALLOWED ON BEACH
800-551-6949   Face Rock State Scenic Viewpoint
                LEASHED DOGS ALLOWED ON BEACH
                Seven Devils State Recreation Area
                LEASHED DOGS ALLOWED ON BEACH

Brookings   Crissy Field State Recreation Area
800-551-6949   **LEASHED DOGS ALLOWED ON BEACH**
541-469-2021   Harris Beach State Park
                LEASHED DOGS ALLOWED ON BEACH
800-551-6949   McVay Rock State Recreation Area
                LEASHED DOGS ALLOWED ON BEACH

Brookings 800-551-6949	Samuel H. Boardman State Scenic Corridor **LEASHED DOGS ALLOWED ON BEACH** Winchuck State Recreation Area **LEASHED DOGS ALLOWED ON BEACH**
Coos Bay 800-551-6949 541-888-3732 541-888-4902	Cape Arago State Park **LEASHED DOGS ALLOWED ON BEACH** Shore Acres State Park *NO DOGS ALLOWED OUTSIDE VEHICLE* Sunset Bay State Park **LEASHED DOGS ALLOWED ON BEACH**
Florence 541-547-3416 800-551-6949	Carl G. Washburne Memorial State Park **LEASHED DOGS ALLOWED ON BEACH** Devil's Elbow State Park **LEASHED DOGS ALLOWED ON BEACH** Muriel O. Ponsler State Scenic Viewpoint **LEASHED DOGS ALLOWED ON BEACH**
Gold Beach 800-551-6949	Cape Sebastian State Scenic Corridor **LEASHED DOGS ALLOWED ON BEACH** Otter Point State Recreation Area **LEASHED DOGS ALLOWED ON BEACH** Pistol River State Scenic Viewpoint **LEASHED DOGS ALLOWED ON BEACH**
Port Orford 541-332-6774	Cape Blanco State Park **LEASHED DOGS ALLOWED ON BEACH**

"If you pick up a starving dog and make him prosperous,
he will not bite you; that is the principal
difference between a dog and a man."
-Mark Twain

CENTRAL COAST

Depoe Bay 800-551-6949	Depoe Bay State Park **LEASHED DOGS ALLOWED ON BEACH** Fogarty Creek State Park **LEASHED DOGS ALLOWED ON BEACH**
Lincoln City 800-551-6949 541-994-3070	D River State Recreation Area **LEASHED DOGS ALLOWED ON BEACH** Gleneden Beach State Recreation Area **LEASHED DOGS ALLOWED ON BEACH** Roads End Beach **LEASHED DOGS ALLOWED ON BEACH**
Newport 800-551-6949 541-265-9278 800-551-6949 541-867-7415 800-551-6949	Agate Beach State Recreation Area **LEASHED DOGS ALLOWED ON BEACH** Beverly Beach State Park **LEASHED DOGS ALLOWED ON BEACH** Devils Punchbowl State Natural Area **LEASHED DOGS ALLOWED ON BEACH** Lost Creek State Park **LEASHED DOGS ALLOWED ON BEACH** Ona Beach State Park **LEASHED DOGS ALLOWED ON BEACH** Seal Rock State Recreation Area **LEASHED DOGS ALLOWED ON BEACH** South Beach State Park **LEASHED DOGS ALLOWED ON BEACH** Yaquina Bay State Park **LEASHED DOGS ALLOWED ON BEACH**
Waldport 541-563-3220 800-551-6949	Beachside Recreational Site **LEASHED DOGS ALLOWED ON BEACH** Driftwood Beach State Recreation Area **LEASHED DOGS ALLOWED ON BEACH** Governor Patterson State Park **LEASHED DOGS ALLOWED ON BEACH**
Yachats 800-551-6949	Neptune State Scenic Viewpoint **LEASHED DOGS ALLOWED ON BEACH** Smelt Sands State Recreation Area **LEASHED DOGS ALLOWED ON BEACH** Stonefield Beach State Recreation Area **LEASHED DOGS ALLOWED ON BEACH** Yachats Ocean Road State Natural Site **LEASHED DOGS ALLOWED ON BEACH**

NORTH COAST

Astoria 503-861-1671	Fort Stevens State Park **LEASHED DOGS ALLOWED ON BEACH**
Cannon Beach 800-551-6949	Arcadia Beach State Recreation Area **LEASHED DOGS ALLOWED ON BEACH** Ecola State Park
503-436-2844	**LEASHED DOGS ALLOWED ON BEACH** High Point State Recreation Area
800-551-6949	**LEASHED DOGS ALLOWED ON BEACH** Oswald West State Park **LEASHED DOGS ALLOWED ON BEACH** Tolovana Beach State Recreation Area **LEASHED DOGS ALLOWED ON BEACH**
Gearhart 800-551-6949	Del Ray Beach State Recreational Area **LEASHED DOGS ALLOWED ON BEACH**
Manzanita 503-368-5154	Nehalem Bay State Park **LEASHED DOGS ALLOWED ON BEACH**
Neskowin 800-551-6949	Neskowin Beach State Recreation Area **LEASHED DOGS ALLOWED ON BEACH**
Pacific City 800-551-6949	Bob Straub State Park **LEASHED DOGS ALLOWED ON BEACH**
Rockaway Beach 800-551-6949	Manhattan Beach State Recreation Area **LEASHED DOGS ALLOWED ON BEACH**
Tillamook 800-551-6949 503-842-4981	Cape Meares State Park **LEASHED DOGS ALLOWED ON BEACH** Cape Lookout State Park **LEASHED DOGS ALLOWED ON BEACH**
800-551-6949	Oceanside Beach State Recreation Area **LEASHED DOGS ALLOWED ON BEACH**

"Properly trained, a man can be dog's best friend."
-Corey Ford

Washington

Dogs on leash are allowed in all Washington state parks but not in many swimming areas around Puget Sound. The uncrowded Pacific Coast beaches are some of the dog-friendliest in America - even Olympic National Park, which bans dogs from almost all of its 632,324 acres, opens some of its remote coastal beaches to dogs.

Recommended Tail-Friendly Beaches

- **Long Beach Peninsula.** Miles of wide open sand on the Pacific Ocean and county officials who promise not to enforce leash laws on the beach providing your dog is well-behaved. Now that is a deal all dog owners can live with!

- **North Beach Point.** On the Olympic Peninsula here you get acccess to the shoreline of Juan de Fuca Strait and Fort Worden State Park. Great for boat watching, beach combing, dog walking and sunsets.

- **Warren G. Magnuson Park (Sand Point).** Seattle's second-largest park at 350 acres features a mile-long shoreline on Lake Washington. It is freshwater but it is also the only dog beach in Seattle. Plenty of convenient parking in this former Navy facility.

PACIFIC OCEAN

Forks	First Beach
360-374-2558	**LEASHED DOGS ALLOWED ON BEACH**
360-565-3147	Olympic National Park
	DOGS ARE ALLOWED ON THE BEACH FROM RIALTO BEACH NORTH TO ELLEN CREEK AND AT KALALOCH NORTH TO THE HOH RIVER
360-374-2558	Second Beach
	LEASHED DOGS ALLOWED ON BEACH
	Third Beach
	LEASHED DOGS ALLOWED ON BEACH
Hoquiam	Griffith-Priday Ocean State Park
360-902-8844	**LEASHED DOGS ALLOWED ON BEACH**

Ilwaco 360-642-3145	Beerd's Hollow Beach **LEASHED DOGS ALLOWED ON BEACH** Fort Canby State Park **LEASHED DOGS ALLOWED ON BEACH**
Long Beach 800-451-2542	10th Street Access **LEASHED DOGS ALLOWED ON BEACH** Bolsted Beach Access **LEASHED DOGS ALLOWED ON BEACH** Seaview Beach Access **LEASHED DOGS ALLOWED ON BEACH**
Ocean Park 360-902-8844	Pacific Pines State Park **LEASHED DOGS ALLOWED ON BEACH**
Ocean Shores 360-902-8844 360-289-3331	Damon Point State Park **LEASHED DOGS ALLOWED ON BEACH** Ocean City State Park **LEASHED DOGS ALLOWED ON BEACH** Pacific Beach State Park **LEASHED DOGS ALLOWED ON BEACH** Town Beach **LEASHED DOGS ALLOWED ON BEACH AND CAN RUN FREE ONCE YOU ARE PAST THE DUNES AND ON THE SAND**
Oysterville 360-902-8844	Leadbetter Point State Park **LEASHED DOGS ALLOWED ON BEACH** Oysterville Beach **LEASHED DOGS ALLOWED ON BEACH**
Westport 360-902-8844	Grayland Beach State Park **LEASHED DOGS ALLOWED ON BEACH** Twin Harbors Beach State Park **LEASHED DOGS ALLOWED ON BEACH** Westport Light State Park **LEASHED DOGS ALLOWED ON BEACH**

"Children are for people who can't have dogs."
-Anonymous

INLAND

Belfair
360-902-8844

Belfair State Park
**LEASHED DOGS ALLOWED ON BEACH
BUT NOT IN SWIMMING AREAS**
Twanoh State Park
**LEASHED DOGS ALLOWED ON BEACH
BUT NOT IN SWIMMING AREAS**

Bellingham
360-902-8844

Larrbee State Park
**LEASHED DOGS ALLOWED ON BEACH
BUT NOT IN SWIMMING AREAS**

Blaine
360-902-8844

Birch Bay State Park
**LEASHED DOGS ALLOWED ON BEACH
BUT NOT IN SWIMMING AREAS**

Blake Island
360-902-8844

Blake Island State Park
**LEASHED DOGS ALLOWED ON BEACH
BUT NOT IN SWIMMING AREAS**

Bremerton
360-902-8844

Illahee State Park
**LEASHED DOGS ALLOWED ON BEACH
BUT NOT IN SWIMMING AREAS**

Brinnon
360-902-8844

Dosewallips State Park
**LEASHED DOGS ALLOWED ON BEACH
BUT NOT IN SWIMMING AREAS**

Burlington
360-902-8844

Bay View State Park
**LEASHED DOGS ALLOWED ON BEACH
BUT NOT IN SWIMMING AREAS**

Coupeville
360-902-8844

Fort Casey State Park
**LEASHED DOGS ALLOWED ON BEACH
BUT NOT IN SWIMMING AREAS**
Fort Ebey State Park
**LEASHED DOGS ALLOWED ON BEACH
BUT NOT IN SWIMMING AREAS**

Des Moines
360-902-8844

Saltwater State Park
**LEASHED DOGS ALLOWED ON BEACH
BUT NOT IN SWIMMING AREAS**

Federal Way
360-902-8844

Dash Point State Park
**LEASHED DOGS ALLOWED ON BEACH
BUT NOT IN SWIMMING AREAS**

Freeland
360-902-8844

South Whidbey Island State Park
**LEASHED DOGS ALLOWED ON BEACH
BUT NOT IN SWIMMING AREAS**

Gig Harbor 253-265-3606	Kopachuck State Park **LEASHED DOGS ALLOWED ON BEACH BUT NOT IN SWIMMING AREAS**
Harstine Island 360-902-8844	Jarrell Cove State Park **LEASHED DOGS ALLOWED ON BEACH BUT NOT IN SWIMMING AREAS**
Hope Island 360-902-8844	Hope Island State Park *NO DOGS ALLOWED IN PARK*
Lopez Island 360-902-8844	Spencer Spit State Park **LEASHED DOGS ALLOWED ON BEACH BUT NOT IN SWIMMING AREAS**
Marrowstone Island 360-902-8844	Mystery Bay State Park **LEASHED DOGS ALLOWED ON BEACH BUT NOT IN SWIMMING AREAS**
Mukilteo 360-902-8844	Mulkiteo State Park **LEASHED DOGS ALLOWED ON BEACH BUT NOT IN SWIMMING AREAS**
Oak Harbor 360-902-8844	Deception Pass State Park **LEASHED DOGS ALLOWED ON BEACH BUT NOT IN SWIMMING AREAS** Joseph Whidbey State Park **LEASHED DOGS ALLOWED ON BEACH BUT NOT IN SWIMMING AREAS**
Olympia 360-902-8844	Tolmic State Park **LEASHED DOGS ALLOWED ON BEACH BUT NOT IN SWIMMING AREAS**
Port Angeles 360-417-2291	Clallam Bay Spit Beach County Park **LEASHED DOGS ALLOWED ON BEACH** Freshwater Bay **LEASHED DOGS ALLOWED ON BEACH** Pillar Point County Park **LEASHED DOGS ALLOWED ON BEACH** Salt Creek State Park **LEASHED DOGS ALLOWED ON BEACH**
Port Townsend 360-902-8844	Fort Worden State Park **LEASHED DOGS ALLOWED ON BEACH BUT NOT IN SWIMMING AREAS**
Port Walow 360-902-8844	Shine Tidelands State Park **LEASHED DOGS ALLOWED ON BEACH BUT NOT IN SWIMMING AREAS**

Poulsbo 360-779-3205	Kitsap Memorial State Park **LEASHED DOGS ALLOWED ON BEACH** **BUT NOT IN SWIMMING AREAS**
Purdy 360-902-8844	Penrose Point State Park **LEASHED DOGS ALLOWED ON BEACH** **BUT NOT IN SWIMMING AREAS**
Seattle 206-296-8359	Alki Beach *NO DOGS ALLOWED ON SEATTLE BEACHES* Carkeek Park *NO DOGS ALLOWED ON SEATTLE BEACHES* Constellation ParK *NO DOGS ALLOWED ON SEATTLE BEACHES* Des Moines Beach Park *NO DOGS ALLOWED ON SEATTLE BEACHES* Lincoln Park *NO DOGS ALLOWED ON SEATTLE BEACHES* Richmond Beach *NO DOGS ALLOWED ON SEATTLE BEACHES* Seahurst Park *NO DOGS ALLOWED ON SEATTLE BEACHES*
Sequim 360-417-2291 360-683-5847 360-417-2291 360-902-8844	Cline Spit Beach County Park **LEASHED DOGS ALLOWED ON BEACH** Dungeness Recreation Area **LEASHED DOGS ALLOWED ON BEACH** Panorama Vista Access **LEASHED DOGS ALLOWED ON BEACH** Port Williams County Park **LEASHED DOGS ALLOWED ON BEACH** Sequim Bay State Park **LEASHED DOGS ALLOWED ON BEACH** **BUT NOT IN SWIMMING AREAS**
Shelton 360-902-8844	Potlatch State Park **LEASHED DOGS ALLOWED ON BEACH** **BUT NOT IN SWIMMING AREAS**
Silverdale 360-902-8844	Scenic Beach State Park **LEASHED DOGS ALLOWED ON BEACH** **BUT NOT IN SWIMMING AREAS**
South Point 360-902-8844	Fort Ward State Park **LEASHED DOGS ALLOWED ON BEACH** **BUT NOT IN SWIMMING AREAS**
Tacoma 360-902-8844	Joemma Beach State Park **LEASHED DOGS ALLOWED ON BEACH** **BUT NOT IN SWIMMING AREAS**

Your Dog On The Great Lakes Beaches...

Lake Superior

Possessing the largest surface area of any freshwater lake in the world, there is enough water in Lake Superior to easily fill the other four Great Lakes to overflowing. Lake Superior is known for its cold water and rugged shoreline but there are some sandy beaches scattered across its 300 or so miles of southern shores. Other beaches are more of the cobble variety. Most of the shoreline is sparsely populated which bodes well for finding a dog-friendly beach.

Recommended Tail-Friendly Beaches

🐾 **Pictured Rocks National Lakeshore.** The mineral-stained cliffs on the south shore of Lake Superior were preserved as America's first national lakeshore in 1966. Along the 40 miles of parkland are day hikes leading to clifftops and cobble beaches through hardwood forests and windswept dunes. Less than one mile off-shore at the western end of the Pictured Rocks is Grand Island, the largest island in the southern waters of Lake Superior. Leashed dogs ride free on the ferry to the 22-square mile island. Sandy beaches and dramtic shorelines await.

MICHIGAN

Pictured Rocks National Lakeshore
906-387-2607 **AT GRAND MARAIS, LEASHED DOGS ALLOWED ON BEACH FROM TWELVEMILE BEACH CAMPGROUND TO AU SABLE LIGHTHOUSE; AT MUNISING, DOGS ALLOWED ON BEACH AT MINERS BEACH EXCEPT ON LAKESHORE TRAIL AT EAST END OF BEACH; DOGS ALLOWED ON SAND POINT UNTIL TRAIL BEGINS TO CLIMB CLIFFS**

Big Bay Burns Landing Beach
906-225-8150 **DOGS ALLOWED ON BEACH**

Brimley Brimley State Park
906-482-0278 *NO DOGS ALLOWED ON BEACH*

Copper Harbor Keweenaw Point
800-338-7982 **DOGS ALLOWED ON BEACH**

Eagle Harbor
800-338-7982

Great Sand Bay
NO DOGS ALLOWED ON BEACH

Eagle River
800-338-7982

Five Mile Point
DOGS ALLOWED ON BEACH

Grand Marais
906-494-2381

Woodland Park
LEASHED DOGS ALLOWED ON BEACH

Hancock
906-482-0278

F.J. McLain State Park
NO DOGS ALLOWED ON BEACH

Marquette
906-228-0460

McCartys Cove
NO DOGS ALLOWED ON BEACH
South Beach
NO DOGS ALLOWED ON BEACH
Tourist Park
NO DOGS ALLOWED ON BEACH

Munising
906-387-3700

Grand Island National Recreation Area
LEASHED DOGS ALLOWED ON BEACH

Paradise
906-492-3219

Whitefish Point
DOGS ALLOWED ON REMOTE BEACHES FROM POINT ON WEST, ACCESSED BY UNDEVELOPED ROADS

Toivola
800-338-7982

Agate Beach
DOGS ALLOWED ON BEACH

WISCONSIN

Ashland
800-284-9484

Bayview Park
LEASHED DOGS ALLOWED ON BEACH
Kreher Beach
LEASHED DOGS ALLOWED ON BEACH
Maslowski Beach
LEASHED DOGS ALLOWED ON BEACH

Bayfield
800-447-4094

Broad Street Beach
DOGS ALLOWED ON BEACH

Superior
715-392-2773

Barker's Island
NO DOGS ALLOWED ON BEACH

MINNESOTA

Duluth
218-723-3337

Park Point Beach
LEASHED DOGS ALLOWED ON BEACH

Lake Michigan

Dogs will have to admire the spectacular dunes and sandy beaches of the eastern shore of Lake Michigan mostly from the car as dogs are not allowed on Michigan state beaches and most county and town beaches. In-season, the metropolises of Indiana, Illinois and Wisconsin are even more restrictive. Your best bets to dip into Lake Michigan, the only Great Lake totally within the United States, are the national lakeshores and the state parks of Wisconsin's Door County.

Recommended Tail-Friendly Beaches

🐾 **Sleeping Bear Dunes National Lakeshore.** Your dog isn't allowed to make the Dune Climb up a mountain of sand but she may thank you for that. Otherwise dogs are welcome on Sleeping Bear Dunes National Lakeshore trails on the eastern shore. In the north section of the park most of the starch has been taken out of the Lake Michigan waves here for gentle canine swimming. More adventurous dog paddlers will want to test the frisky waves in the southernmost Platte Plains section. You have your choice of trails here to choose how much you want to hike before reaching the surf.

🐾 **Indiana Dunes National Lakeshore.** The 25 miles of southern Lake Michigan shoreline is a place of striking contrasts. Growing zones clash here so in the shadow of the industrial surroundings of Gary, Indiana southern dogwoods mix with arctic bearberry and northern conifer forests thrive along cacti. The native plant diversity here ranks 7th among all National Parklands. Standing between the waters of Lake Michigan and your dog is the 123-foot Mt. Baldy sandpile. If you take your time, even older dogs can make it to the top or, if your dog is in a hurry to get to the water, you can hike a trail around Mt. Baldy directly to the beach.

MICHIGAN - UPPER PENINSULA

Cedar River
906-863-9747

J.W. Wells State Park
NO DOGS ALLOWED ON BEACH

Escanaba
906-789-7862
906-786-4141

Fuller Park
LEASHED DOGS ALLOWED ON BEACH
Ludington Park
LEASHED DOGS ALLOWED ON BEACH

Garden Corners
906-644-2603

Fayette Historic State Park
NO DOGS ALLOWED ON BEACH

Gladstone
906-786-9234

VanCleve Park
DOGS ALLOWED ON CAMPGROUND AND PARK BEACHES BUT NOT IN SWIMMING BEACH

Manistique
906-341-5010

Town Beach
LEASHED DOGS ALLOWED ON BEACH

St. Ignace
906-643-8717

Lake Michigan Sand Dunes
DOGS ALLOWED ON BEACH

MICHIGAN - NORTHWEST

Sleeping Bear Dunes National Lakeshore
231-326-5134

DOGS ALLOWED ON BEACH EXCEPT ON PLATTE POINTE BEACH, NORTH MANTIOU ISLAND, SOUTH MANITOU ISLAND AND D.H. DAY CAMPGROUND BEACH

Acme
231-938-1350

Acme Township Beach
NO DOGS ALLOWED ON BEACH
Bayside Beach
NO DOGS ALLOWED ON BEACH
Dock Street Beach
LEASHED DOGS ALLOWED ON BEACH
Tony Gilroy Township Park
NO DOGS ALLOWED ON BEACH

Beaver Island
231-448-2205

Beaver Island Public Beach
LEASHED DOGS ALLOWED ON BEACH
Bill Wagner Memorial Campground Beach
LEASHED DOGS ALLOWED ON BEACH
Harbor Beach
LEASHED DOGS ALLOWED ON BEACH
Iron Ore Beach
LEASHED DOGS ALLOWED ON BEACH

Charlevoix 231-547-6641 231-547-2101	Fisherman's Island State Park *NO DOGS ALLOWED ON BEACH* Lake Michigan Beach **DOGS ALLOWED ON BEACH** Mt. McSauba Beach **DOGS ALLOWED ON BEACH** Peninsula Municipal Park Beach **DOGS ALLOWED ON BEACH**
Eastport 231-599-2712	Barnes Park *NO DOGS ALLOWED ON BEACH*
Empire 231-271-9895	Empire Beach *NO DOGS ALLOWED ON BEACH* Esch Road Beach *NO DOGS ALLOWED ON BEACH*
Glen Arbor 231-271-9895	Glen Arbor Municipal Beach *NO DOGS ALLOWED ON BEACH*
Harbor Springs 231-526-7999	Thorne Swift Nature Preserve *NO DOGS ALLOWED ON BEACH* Zoll Street Beach **DOGS ALLOWED ON BEACH** Zorn Park *NO DOGS ALLOWED ON BEACH*
Leland 231-271-9895	Leland Municipal Beach *NO DOGS ALLOWED ON BEACH*
Mackinaw City 231-436-5574 231-436-5381	Cecil Bay Beach **DOGS ALLOWED ON BEACH** Wilderness State Park *NO DOGS ALLOWED ON BEACH*
Northport 231-922-5270 231-271-9895	Leelanau State Park *NO DOGS ALLOWED ON BEACH* Northport Beach *NO DOGS ALLOWED ON BEACH* Peterson Park *NO DOGS ALLOWED ON BEACH*
Old Mission 231-223-7322 231-223-7897	Haserot Beach **LEASHED DOGS ALLOWED ON BEACH** Old Mission Lighthouse Park Beach **LEASHED DOGS ALLOWED ON BEACH**
Petoskey 231-347-4150 231-347-2311	Magnus City Beach *DOGS NOT ALLOWED IN SWIMMING AREAS* Petoskey State Park *NO DOGS ALLOWED ON BEACH*

Suttons Bay 231-271-5077	Suttons Bay Municipal Beach *NO DOGS ALLOWED ON BEACH*
Traverse City 231-922-4480	Bowers Harbor Beach **LEASHED DOGS ALLOWED ON BEACH BUT NOT IN DESIGNATED SWIMMING AREAS** Bryant Park **LEASHED DOGS ALLOWED ON BEACH BUT NOT IN DESIGNATED SWIMMING AREAS**
231-922-4903	Clinch Park Beach **LEASHED DOGS ALLOWED ON BEACH BUT NOT IN DESIGNATED SWIMMING AREAS**
231-922-4480	East Bay Park Beach **LEASHED DOGS ALLOWED ON BEACH BUT NOT IN DESIGNATED SWIMMING AREAS**
231-922-5270	Traverse City State Park *NO DOGS ALLOWED ON BEACH*
231-922-4480	West End Beach **LEASHED DOGS ALLOWED ON BEACH BUT NOT IN DESIGNATED SWIMMING AREAS**
Yuba 231-938-1350	Sayler Park *NO DOGS ALLOWED ON BEACH*

MICHIGAN - CENTRAL WEST

Arcadia 877-626-4783	Arcadia Park *NO DOGS ALLOWED ON BEACH*
Elberta 231-352-7251	Elberta Bluffs *NO DOGS ALLOWED ON BEACH*
Grand Haven 616-842-3210	Grand Haven City Beach **NO DOGS ALLOWED ON BEACH BETWEEN THE SWIMMING BUOYS BETWEEN MEMORIAL DAY AND LABOR DAY; LEASHED DOGS ALLOWED ANYTIME SOUTH OF SOUTHERLY BUOY**
616-798-3711	Grand Haven State Park NO DOGS ALLOWED ON BEACH
616-646-8117	Kirk Park **DOGS ALLOWED ON BEACH OCT 1 TO MAY 1** North Beach Park **DOGS ALLOWED ON BEACH OCT 1 TO MAY 1**

Holland 616-355-1300	Riley Beach *NO DOGS ALLOWED ON BEACH*
Ludington 877-420-6618	Buttersville Beach **DOGS ALLOWED ON BEACH** Loomis Street Boat Launch **DOGS ALLOWED ON SMALL BEACH ON EITHER SIDE OF LAUNCH**
231-843-8671	Ludington State Park *NO DOGS ALLOWED ON BEACH*
877-420-6618	Stearns Park Beach *NO DOGS ALLOWED IN PARK OR ON BEACH*
Manistee 231-723-2575	Fifth Avenue Beach **LEASHED DOGS ALLOWED ON BEACH** First Street Beach **LEASHED DOGS ALLOWED ON BEACH**
231-723-2211	Lake Michigan Recreation Area **LEASHED DOGS ALLOWED ON BEACH EXCEPT IN RECREATION AREAS**
231-723-7422	Orchard Beach State Park *NO DOGS ALLOWED ON BEACH*
Montague 231-893-4585 231-894-4881	Medbury Park-North Side **DOGS ALLOWED ON BEACH** Meinert County Park **DOGS ALLOWED ON BEACH**
231-893-4585	White Lake Channel **DOGS ALLOWED ON BEACH**
Muskegon 231-724-6704	Kruse Park **DOGS ALLOWED ON BEACH** Pere Marquette Beach **DOGS ALLOWED ON SOUTH END OF BEACH AT WEST END OF SHERMAN AVENUE**
North Muskegon 231-744-3480	Muskegon State Park *NO DOGS ALLOWED ON BEACH*
Norton Shores 231-798-3711	P.J. Hoffmaster State Park *NO DOGS ALLOWED ON BEACH*
Pentwater 231-869-2051	Charles Mears State Park *NO DOGS ALLOWED ON BEACH*
Whitehall 231-893-4585	Duck Lake Channel Beach **DOGS ALLOWED ON BEACH** Whitehall River Lighthouse Museum Beach
231-744-3480	**DOGS ALLOWED ON BEACH**

MICHIGAN - SOUTHWEST

Benton Harbor
616-983-7111 x8435

Jean Klock Park
NO DOGS ALLOWED ON BEACH
Rocky Gap Park
NO DOGS ALLOWED ON BEACH

Bridgman
616-465-3406

Weko Beach
NO DOGS ALLOWED ON BEACH

Covert
269-764-1421

Covert Township Park
NO DOGS ALLOWED ON BEACH

Hagar Shores
616-925-6301

Roadside Park
LEASHED DOGS ALLOWED ON BEACH

Holland
616-399-9390
800-506-1299

Holland State Park
NO DOGS ALLOWED ON BEACH
Tunnel Park
NO DOGS ALLOWED ON BEACH

New Buffalo
269-469-1011

Township & City Beaches
NO DOGS ALLOWED ON BEACH

Saugatuck
616-867-1418
616-637-2788

Oval Beach Recreation Area
NO DOGS ALLOWED ON BEACH
Saugatuck Dunes State Park
NO DOGS ALLOWED ON BEACH

Sawyer
616-426-4013

Warren Dunes State Park
*NO DOGS ALLOWED ON BEACH BUT
CAN GO ON TRAILS*

South Haven
269-637-0700

616-637-2788

Dyckman Park Beach
NO DOGS ALLOWED ON BEACH
North Beach
NO DOGS ALLOWED ON BEACH
Oak Street Beach
NO DOGS ALLOWED ON BEACH
Packard Beach
NO DOGS ALLOWED ON BEACH
South Beach
NO DOGS ALLOWED ON BEACH
Van Buren State Park
NO DOGS ALLOWED ON BEACH

St. Joseph 616-983-6325	Lions Beach *NO DOGS ALLOWED ON BEACH* Silver Beach *NO DOGS ALLOWED ON BEACH BUT CAN* *GO ON SIDEWALKS AND PIER* Tiscornia Park *NO DOGS ALLOWED ON BEACH*
Stevensville 616-429-1802 616-426-4013 616-429-1802	Glenlord Beach *NO DOGS ALLOWED ON BEACH* Grand Mere State Park *NO DOGS ALLOWED ON BEACH* Township Beach *NO DOGS ALLOWED ON BEACH*
Union Pier 616-395-1525	Chikaming Township Beach *LOCAL RESIDENT DOGS ONLY ON BEACH* Lake Minchigan Beach *NO DOGS ALLOWED ON BEACH*

INDIANA

Indiana Dunes National Lakeshore

219-926-7561 x225	**DURING THE SUMMER LEASHED DOGS ALLOWED ON THE EASTERNMOST BEACHES - MT. BALDY AND CENTRAL AVENUE; AFTER SEPT 30 OTHER BEACHES OPEN TO DOGS**
Chesterton 219-926-1952	Indiana Dunes State Park *NO DOGS ALLOWED IN THE SWIMMING AREAS*
Gary 219-885-7407	Lake Street *NO DOGS ALLOWED IN THE SWIMMING AREAS* Marquette Park *NO DOGS ALLOWED IN THE SWIMMING AREAS* Wells Street *NO DOGS ALLOWED IN THE SWIMMING AREAS*
Michigan City 219-873-1506	Washington Park *NO DOGS ALLOWED ON BEACH OR PARK*
Whiting 219-659-7700	Whihala Beach County Park *NO DOGS ALLOWED ON BEACH OR PARK*

ILLINOIS

Beach Park 847-746-1770	North Marina *NO DOGS ALLOWED ON BEACH* North Point *NO DOGS ALLOWED ON BEACH*
Chicago 312-742-DOGS	City Beaches *NO DOGS ALLOWED ON CHICAGO BEACHES* Belmont Beach **THIS IS NOT AN OFFICIAL CHICAGO BEACH SO DOGS ARE ALLOWED ON THIS SMALL BEACH IN A FENCED AREA** Montrose Avenue Beach **THE ONLY OFFICIAL DOG BEACH IN CHICAGO**
Evanston 847-492-7082	Clark Street Beach *NO DOGS ALLOWED ON BEACH* Dog Beach **DOGS ALLOWED ON THIS BEACH AT CHURCH STREET BUT A BEACH TOKEN IS REQUIRED FOR NON-RESIDENTS FROM MAY TO OCT THAT COSTS $80-$100** Lighthouse Beach
847-492-7082	*NO DOGS ALLOWED ON BEACH*
Lake Bluff 847-283-0850	Sunrise Beach **DOGS ALLOWED IN SEASON WITH A BEACH PASS**
Lake Forest 847-615-4207	Lake Forest Beach *NO DOGS ALLOWED ON BEACH*
Waukegan 847-336-1044	Waukegan Municipal Beach *NO DOGS ALLOWED ON BEACH*
Wilmette 847-256-9660	Gillson Park **NO DOGS ALLOWED IN PARK BUT CAN GO ON BEACH AT THE SOUTHERN TIP OF THE PARK BETWEEN THE PIER AND HARBOR MOUTH; NON-RESIDENT TOKEN REQUIRED IN SEASON AT COST OF $150**

Winnetka 847-501-2040	Elder Beach **DOGS ARE ALLOWED ON BEACH SOUTH OF ELDER LANE ONLY; TOKENS REQUIRED IN-SEASON** Maple Beach *NO DOGS ALLOWED ON BEACH* Tower Beach *NO DOGS ALLOWED ON BEACH*
Zion 847-662-4828	Illinois Beach State Park *NO DOGS ALLOWED ON THE BEACH OR NATURE PRESERVE; CAN BE IN PICNIC AREAS, CAMPGROUND, AND ON TRAILS*

WISCONSIN -SOUTHEAST

Cleveland 920-693-8256	Hika Park *NO DOGS ALLOWED ON BEACH*
Kenosha 262-653-4080	Alford Park *NO DOGS ALLOWED ON BEACH* Eichelman Beach *NO DOGS ALLOWED ON BEACH* Pennoyer Park *NO DOGS ALLOWED ON BEACH* Simmons Island Park *NO DOGS ALLOWED ON BEACH* Southport Park *NO DOGS ALLOWED ON BEACH*
Manitowoc 920-683-4530	Red Arrow Park *NO DOGS ALLOWED ON BEACH*
Milwaukee 414-257-6100	Bender Beach *NO DOGS ALLOWED ON BEACH* Bradford Beach *NO DOGS ALLOWED ON BEACH* Doctor's Park Beach *NO DOGS ALLOWED ON BEACH* Grant Beach *NO DOGS ALLOWED ON BEACH* McKinley Beach *NO DOGS ALLOWED ON BEACH* South Shore Beach *NO DOGS ALLOWED ON BEACH*
Racine 262-636-9101	North Beach *NO DOGS ALLOWED ON BEACH*

Sheboygan	Kohler-Andrae State Park
920-451-4080	**NO DOGS ALLOWED ON SWIMMING BEACH BUT DOGS ARE ALLOWED ON THE BEACH AREA NORTH OF THE PARK NATURE CENTER**
920-459-3366	Sheboygan Lakefront
	NO DOGS ALLOWED ON BEACH
Two Rivers	Neshotah Beach
920-793-5592	*NO DOGS ALLOWED ON BEACH*
920-794-7480	Point Beach State Forest
	LEASHED DOGS ALLOWED ON BEACH

WISCONSIN - NORTHEAST

Algoma	Crescent Beach
920-487-5203	*NO DOGS ALLOWED ON BEACH OR ANY ALGOMA PARKS*
Baileys Harbor	Anclam Park
920-839-2366	**LEASHED DOGS ALLOWED ON BEACH**
	Baileys Harbor County Park
	LEASHED DOGS ALLOWED ON BEACH
Egg Harbor	Egg Harbor Beach
920-743-6141	**LEASHED DOGS ALLOWED ON BEACH**
	Murphy Park
	LEASHED DOGS ALLOWED ON BEACH
Ellison Bay	Ellison Bay Beach
920-743-4456	**LEASHED DOGS ALLOWED ON BEACH**
920-854-2500	Newport State Park
	DOGS CAN USE THE BEACH AT THE NORTH BEACH AT THE END OF EUROPE BAY ROAD. MUST BE LEASHED ON THE BEACH BUT CAN GO OFF LEASH IN WATER
Ephraim	Ephraim Village Beach
920-854-5501	*NO DOGS ALLOWED ON BEACH*
Fish Creek	Fish Creek Beach
920-743-4456	**LEASHED DOGS ALLOWED ON BEACH**
	Nicolet Bay Beach
	LEASHED DOGS ALLOWED ON BEACH
920-868-3258	Peninsula State Park
	NO DOGS ALLOWED ON BEACH

Jacksonport 920-823-2314 920-823-2400	Lakeside Park *NO DOGS ALLOWED ON BEACH* Whitefish Dunes State Park **DOGS ALLOWED ON BEACH**
Sister Bay 920-854-4118	Sister Bay Park **LEASHED DOGS ALLOWED ON BEACH**
Sturgeon Bay 920-743-6246	Otumba Park *NO DOGS ALLOWED ON BEACH* Sunset Park *NO DOGS ALLOWED ON BEACH*
Washington 920-847-2522 920-847-2235 920-847-2522	Gislason Public Beach **LEASHED DOGS ALLOWED ON BEACH** Percy Johnson Memorial County Park **LEASHED DOGS ALLOWED ON BEACH** Rock Island State Park *NO DOGS ALLOWED ON BEACH* Schoolhouse Beach **LEASHED DOGS ALLOWED ON BEACH** Sand Dune Beach **LEASHED DOGS ALLOWED ON BEACH**

*"They are superior to human beings as companions.
They do not quarrel or argue with you. They never talk about
themselves but listen to you while you talk about yourself, and keep
an appearance of being interested in the conversation."*
-Jerome K. Jerome

Lake Huron

Lake Huron features 3,827 miles of shorline, characterized by shallow water and many sandy beaches. None of this will matter much to your dog, however, since the Lake Huron beaches in Michigan are mostly closed to him.

MICHIGAN

Alpena 989-354-4181	Bay View Park **LEASHED DOGS ALLOWED ON BEACH** Blair Street Park **LEASHED DOGS ALLOWED ON BEACH** Mich-E-Kewis Beach **LEASHED DOGS ALLOWED ON BEACH** Starlight Beach **LEASHED DOGS ALLOWED ON BEACH** Thompson Park **LEASHED DOGS ALLOWED ON BEACH**
Bay City 989-684-3020	Bay City State Park *NO DOGS ALLOWED ON BEACH*
Caseville 989-856-4411	Albert E. Sleepe State Park *NO DOGS ALLOWED ON BEACH*
Cheboygan 231-627-2811	Cheboygan State Park *NO DOGS ALLOWED ON BEACH*
East Tawas 800-55-TAWAS 989-362-5041	East Tawas City Park *NO DOGS ALLOWED ON BEACH* Tawas Point State Park *NO DOGS ALLOWED ON BEACH*
Harrisville 989-724-5126	Harrisville State Park *NO DOGS ALLOWED ON BEACH*
Lakeport 810-327-6224	Lakeport State Park *NO DOGS ALLOWED ON BEACH*
Lexington 810-359-2262	Burtchville Township Park *NO DOGS ON BEACH OR BREAKWALL* Jeddo Road Beach *NO DOGS ON BEACH OR BREAKWALL* Keewahdin Road Beach *NO DOGS ON BEACH OR BREAKWALL* Krafft Road Beach *NO DOGS ON BEACH OR BREAKWALL* Metcalf Road Beach *NO DOGS ON BEACH OR BREAKWALL*

Macinac Island 800-454-5227	Island Beaches **LEASHED DOGS ALLOWED ON ISLAND**
Mackinaw City 800-666-0160	Mackinaw City Beach *NO DOGS ALLOWED ON BEACH*
Oscada 800-235-4625	Oscada Beach *NO DOGS ALLOWED ON BEACH*
Port Austin 989-738-8863	Port Crescent State Park *NO DOGS ALLOWED ON BEACH*
Port Huron 810-739-7322 810-984-9760	Lakeside Beach **DOGS ALLOWED ON BEACH** Lighthouse Park **DOGS ALLOWED ON BEACH**
Rogers City 989-734-2543	P.H. Hoeft State Park *NO DOGS ALLOWED ON BEACH*
St. Ignace 906-643-8717	Kiwanis Beach **DOGS ALLOWED ON BEACH**
Tawas 800-55-TAWAS	Tawas City Park *NO DOGS ALLOWED ON BEACH*

"If there are no dogs in heaven,
then when I die I want to go where they went."
-Anonymous

Lake Erie

Although its shores are the most densely populated of any of the Great Lakes, there is plenty of opportunity for a dog to explore Lake Erie. The smallest of the five lakes, Erie waters average only about 62 feet in depth and warm rapidly in the summer for happy dog paddling.

Recommended Tail-Friendly Beaches

☙ **Presque Isle State Park.** The 3,200-acre peninsula was designated a National Natural Landmark in 1969 and is home to Pennsylvania's most popular state park. Presque Isle is unique in that plant succession from sandy shoreline to climax forest can be seen in less than one mile. Dogs are welcome on all trails but ticks are heavy so avoid the trail fringes. Dogs are not allowed on the swimming beaches but you can hike a little ways up the peninsula past the supervised beaches where dogs can enjoy the energetic waves of Lake Erie.

MICHIGAN

Luna Pier 734-242-3366	City Beach *NO DOGS ALLOWED ON BEACH*
Sterling 734-289-2715	Sterling State Park *NO DOGS ALLOWED ON BEACH*

OHIO

Ashtabula 440-993-7164	Walnut Beach **LEASHED DOGS ALLOWED ON BEACH**
Cleveland 216-881-8141	Cleveland Lakefront Park *NO DOGS ALLOWED ON BEACH* Edgewater Park *NO DOGS ALLOWED ON BEACH* Euclid Beach *NO DOGS ALLOWED ON BEACH*
216-351-6300	Huntington Reserve *NO DOGS ALLOWED ON BEACH*
216-881-8141	Villa Angela *NO DOGS ALLOWED ON BEACH*

Fairport Harbor 440-639-9972	Lakefront Park *NO DOGS ALLOWED ON BEACH*
Geneva 440-466-8400	Geneva State Park *NO DOGS ALLOWED ON BEACH*
Huron 419-433-8487 419-433-7244	Lakefront Park **DOGS ALLOWED ON BEACH** Nickel Plate Beach **DOGS ALLOWED ON BEACH**
Lorain 440-458-5121	Lakeside Landing **LEASHED DOGS ALLOWED ON BEACH**
Marblehead 419-734-4424	East Harbor State Park **LEASHED DOGS ALLOWED ON DESIGNATED PARTS OF BEACH** East Harbor State Park **LEASHED DOGS ALLOWED ON DESIGNATED PARTS OF BEACH**
Mentor 216-881-8141	Headlands Beach State Park *NO DOGS ALLOWED ON BEACH*
Oak Harbor 419-836-7758	Crane Creek State Park *NO DOGS ALLOWED ON BEACH*
Oregon 419-836-7758	Maumee Bay Park *NO DOGS ALLOWED ON BEACH*
Port Clinton 419-732-2206	City Beach **LEASHED DOGS ALLOWED ON MAIN BEACH; EAST AND WEST SIDES DOGS MAY RUN FREE AND IN THE WATER**
Put-in-Bay 419-797-4530	Kelleys Island State Park *NO DOGS ALLOWED ON BEACH* South Bass Island State Park *NO DOGS ALLOWED ON BEACH*
Vermilion 440-967-4477	Main Street Beach **LEASHED DOGS ALLOWED ON BEACH**

PENNSYLVANIA

Erie
814-833-7424

Presque Isle State Park
DOGS ARE NOT ALLOWED IN SWIMMING AREAS, WHICH ARE THE SUPERVISED BEACHES

NEW YORK

Blasdell
716-826-1930

Woodlawn Beach State Park
NO DOGS ALLOWED ON BEACH DURING SUMMER OPERATING HOURS

Brockton
716-792-9214

Lake Erie State Park
LEASHED DOGS ALLOWED ON BEACH BUT NOT IN BATHING AREAS

Dunkirk
716-366-3262

Dunkirk Beach
NO DOGS ALLOWED ON BEACH
Point Gratiot Park
LEASHED DOGS ALLOWED ON BEACH EXCEPT DURING SUMMER FROM 12-6 IN LIFEGUARDED AREAS

Evans
716-947-0970

716-947-5660

Bennett Beach
NO DOGS ALLOWED ON BEACH
Evans Town Park Beach
NO DOGS ALLOWED ON BEACH
Lake Erie Beach
NO DOGS ALLOWED ON BEACH
Wendt Beach
NO DOGS ALLOWED ON BEACH

Irving
716-549-1802

Evangola State Park
LEASHED DOGS ALLOWED ON BEACH BUT NOT IN BATHING AREAS

Silver Creek
716-934-3240

George Borrello Park
LEASHED DOGS ALLOWED ON BEACH

Sunset Bay
716-934-3240

Town Beach
LEASHED DOGS ALLOWED ON BEACH

Westfield
716-326-9243

Barcelona Beach
DOGS ALLOWED ON BEACH

Lake Ontario

Not many people have settled most of the hundreds of miles of shoreline of the south side of Lake Ontario in New York. There aren't many beaches and not many bans on dogs - as long as they don't try to swim with the humans.

NEW YORK

Fair Haven
315-947-5205

Fair Haven Beach State Park
LEASHED DOGS ALLOWED ON BEACH BUT NOT IN BATHING AREAS

Hamlin
585-964-2462

Hamlin Beach State Park
LEASHED DOGS ALLOWED ON BEACH BUT NOT IN BATHING AREAS

Henderson
315-846-5338

Southwick Beach State Park
LEASHED DOGS ALLOWED ON BEACH BUT NOT IN BATHING AREAS

Pulaski
315-298-5737

Selkirk Shores State Park
LEASHED DOGS ALLOWED ON BEACH BUT NOT IN BATHING AREAS

Rochester
716-256-4950

Ontario Beach Park
NO DOGS ALLOWED ON BEACH OR IN PARK

Sackets Harbor
315-646-2239

Westcott Beach State Park
LEASHED DOGS ALLOWED ON BEACH BUT NOT IN BATHING AREAS

Sandy Creek
315-349-3451

Sandy Island Beach
NO DOGS ALLOWED ON BEACH

Texas
315-963-8216

Mexico Point State Park
LEASHED DOGS ALLOWED ON BEACH BUT NOT IN BATHING AREAS

Wilson
716-751-6361

Wilson-Tuscarora State Park
LEASHED DOGS ALLOWED ON BEACH BUT NOT BOARDWALK

Index To States

Printed in the United States
115323LV00001B/148/A

9 780979 707445